Advanced Praise for Ensure

"Profound! A refreshing break from traditional thought around teaching and leading education systems…A must read for every educator!"
—*Marshall Goldsmith, NY Times #1 bestselling author of Triggers, Mojo, and What Got You Here Won't Get You There.*

"This book inspires and shows leaders how they can achieve their transformational goals–it cuts to the core of what 21st century school leadership is all about."
—*Jon Gordon, Best-selling author of The Energy Bus and The Power of Positive Leadership*

"If you want to understand how to maximize your leadership to spark change and increase results in school systems– this book is a must-read. Dr. Sam Nix does a masterful job of establishing a leadership process, packed with practical tools and examples."
—*Dr. Marc Smith, Superintendent of School, Duncanville ISD, 2020 Superintendent of the Year Region 10 - Texas*

"Dr. Sam Nix provides the reader with practical examples and processes for how schools can become true learner-centered environments for students and educators. This book should be a universal required reading in every school!"
—*Betty Burks, Executive Leadership Coach, Former Deputy Superintendent, Author: Stop Fake Work in Education*

"An inspirational, informative book of practical tips that will…empower learners, teachers, and leaders to facilitate more successful learning environments. This is a brilliant book for any educator regardless of their experience."
—*LaTonya Goffney, Ed.D., superintendent, Aldine ISD, and 2017 Texas Superintendent of the Year*

"A masterpiece of strategies for educators toward creating a culture of educational success. This is a great book and a must read for educators at all levels of education."
—*Principal Baruti Kafele, Education Consultant, Author, Retired Principal*

ENSURE EDUCATIONAL
SUCCESS

For Eboni, Stevie, and Sam III

SNIX3

snix3consulting.com

sam@snix3consulting.com

ISBN: 978-1-7378715-1-4 (print)
ISBN: 978-1-7378715-2-1 (ebook)

Ordering Information:
Special discounts are available on quantity purchases by corporations, associations, and others. For details, contact email sam@snix3consulting.com.

TABLE OF CONTENTS

ENSURE EDUCATIONAL
SUCCESS

INNOVATIVE *and* COMMON SENSE STRATEGIES
FOR LEADING A SCHOOL CULTURE WHERE
TEACHERS *and* STUDENTS THRIVE

SAMUEL NIX, ED. D

CHAPTER 1 - TRANSFORMING TRADITION

> "Leadership is not something
> you do to people. It's something you do with people."
>
> — Ken Blanchard

The most hazardous threat to the future is the safety of the past. It is human nature to cling to the familiar and to duplicate actions that have produced favorable results. It is comfortable to rely on the lessons of yesterday for the test of today. But that mindset produces a dependence on the familiar and reduces the ability to leap forward through the wall of uncertainty toward improvement and progress. What is learning if not progress?

If students are *our future*, does it make sense to deploy traditional educational organization and implementation from the past? Nothing is as bad for progress as tradition. Growth demands change. Tradition does not. Therefore, if you are hoping to transform a learning environment, a classroom, your school's academic rating, or your student graduation rate, you must be willing to welcome transformation with open arms. That desire means politely telling tradition to take a seat.

Where to start? The prevailing wisdom used to be to hire people and get out of their way. While that sounded great, I saw throughout my career that new hires often lost their passion as time went on. By the traditional, hands-off approach, these people simply carried on without receiving feedback by which they could improve. Quite simply, I disagreed with that philosophy, and I acted on my own ideas. I ensured a level of support that bucked previous tradition at my district. Specifically, I monitored the level of quality instruction by implementing processes such that I'd meet with teachers after every classroom walkthrough to provide feedback and to monitor quality improvement. And it worked—instead of expending resources plugging gaps and picking up the slack, I kept the engines of all employees firing hot by providing them with the continuous support that they needed.

The Purpose of School

What is the purpose of school? Is it to prepare students for the future? Is it to teach students about themselves and the world around them? The first "traditional" notion I would like to challenge is this: *the purpose of school is not just to teach students.* Millions of dollars are spent each year to train, develop, equip, and provide resources for teachers to become more skilled in their profession. Despite the investment, that particular goal is not the sole purpose of a school's existence. In every single school across America, there is a lot of teaching going on. However, students are not always learning, even though teachers are teaching their hearts out. In fact, there are many students struggling to learn.

The purpose of school is not just to teach students. The purpose of school is to ensure that students *are learning.* Everything we do as educators should always go back to demonstrating evidence of student learning. Schools are supposed to be institutions of learning, not institutions of teaching.

I realized that intention when I was teaching, and it has stayed with me throughout the years. As a very young teacher, I came into a school and requested from other teachers to give me students they deemed "challenging." Some of them were behind grade level, some had reading deficiencies, and most were labeled Special Ed, or 504, which referred to students who had defined disabilities. The more students supported with 504 or Special Ed services a teacher has, the more that teacher has to be knowledgeable of their potential plans to support learning and Individualized Education

Plans (IEPS). The more IEPS a teacher has, the more difficult it becomes to provide instruction to a whole group.

But that concern wasn't the biggest issue. The majority of my students did not enjoy their learning environment. They hated school. What should I have done? I could have dug into what I was taught before starting my teaching career. I could have pondered the textbooks that I spent hours poring over to determine the best way to teach my students so that they could excel.

But I didn't. Instead, I observed. For example, one of my history students struggled to read on grade level. How does one teach complex history material to a young mind who is struggling to read and conceptualize the content? Naturally, my student did not enjoy history or school in general. What the student did enjoy, though, was tapping out beats on the desk with a pencil and freestyling raps to go along with the beats. That kid could recite complex rap songs verbatim and wrote original works as well, right off the top of his head. It takes a smart mind to expertly rhyme words and match the syncopation of pencil percussion.

The student engaged in that activity frequently. Other teachers viewed the behavior as a distraction, and even a reason to send the student out of the classroom with a referral. What some saw as a distraction, I saw as an opportunity. If the student enjoyed rapping and making beats, maybe blending history with rap would make the lessons relevant and interesting. I had an idea. I asked a friend to help me compose music to accompany a rap that I would write pertaining to our next unit of study on the Bill of Rights. I was stepping completely out of my comfort zone with this attempt to delve into a world with which I was unfamiliar. But my passion to ensure the student was learning superseded my pride and fear of failure.

My friend and I worked on the lyrics to that song deep into the early hours of the morning. Satisfied with the end result, I burned the finished product onto a CD and presented it to the student the following day. After listening to the history mix, my student's entire demeanor changed. You could see enthusiasm start to radiate around him. Confident about the material and excited for the test, my student requested another mix for the next section we would be covering. I was not teaching the Bill of Rights to this student. I had discovered a way to ensure learning.

I spent the next five years doing everything I could to make sure every student experienced the best education they could when they set foot into my class. And they did! It had nothing to do with what I taught and everything to do with how my students learned.

Think about it. We all have our own personal styles of learning, right? Some of us are visual learners. Some of us prefer to read over material. Some of us are tactile, kinesthetic learners who need to be immersed in the process. The term "differentiation" is in education, and is often found embedded in well-written lesson plans. Differentiation is the subject of many professional-development sessions. But more than just understanding how students learn, it is about understanding their experiences. It is about tapping into their beliefs. The same is true at any level of a school organization, but to do that takes a commitment to invest the time, energy, and effort that unfortunately some are not willing to make.

Had I not taken an interest in my student's beat-tapping hobby and simply presented the material and tested the student like everyone else, that student would have failed. Quite possibly, he would have had to repeat the grade. What does that kind of failure do to the human spirit? Learning feels out of reach, and students give up.

Traditionally, teachers are taught that their job is to provide the information, resources, and opportunities for students. If students cannot conform to those opportunities or continue to struggle, then the failure is their fault. That technical approach to educating students too often results in frustrated teachers and students.

Unfortunately, we do a really good job teaching the kids who need us the least. The kids who need us the most are the ones who aren't on grade level, who are struggling, who have no parental supervision, who are going hungry, who have discipline problems, and so on. My initial teaching experiences enabled me to learn early on that the traditional way of accomplishing instruction was not working.

We have to step outside of our own perspective, listen with the intent to understand, ask the right questions, and observe before acting on any issues. Easier said than done. Believe me, I know. Despite learning that valuable lesson on the teaching side, I had no idea the biggest lesson was waiting for me in the leadership arena.

A Bigger Impact

There are amazing teachers in schools across America. Those teachers excite students to wake up each and every day to experience what their teacher has in store to inspire, motivate, encourage, and ensure that they learn. Sadly, that same scenario is not the reality in far too many classrooms.

In order for teachers to obtain their certification, they must satisfy the requirements of two exams. The first is a content exam to measure their ability to understand "what" they will be teaching. It is a basic determinant to see if they know enough to *teach* students. The second is a pedagogy exam to measure their ability to understand "who" they will be teaching. It is a basic determinant to see if they know how to *reach* students. We will get into the "art" of ensuring learning in the next chapter, but the premise here is to remember that the most successful educators both reach *and* teach.

Birth of a Leader

When I was teaching, you never knew if you would walk into a classroom and find buckets of ice, or the lights off, or a big ball leaning against the desk. Surprises were the norm, and surprises can be exciting. To engage students, I had to make my class an exciting place to be. So, when a student once asked me, "Why can't every class be like this class?" I knew it was time to expand my influence beyond one classroom.

Once I made the decision to become an assistant principal, I decided to reenroll in school to earn an Administrative Leadership Degree. It was a time-intensive grind that demanded more dedication than anything I'd ever done. After two years, it paid off. There's no better feeling than receiving that phone call in which you're told that you will be given an opportunity to interview for your dream position. I remember the first such call that I received. The interview consisted of 13 people in a room, all of whom were intently focused on my every answer to see if I would be a good fit. I was intimidated. In my head, though, I was sure that I knocked the interview out of the park.

I did not receive the position. And I did not receive the one after that. Or the one after that.

But I refused to quit. I finally earned an assistant principal position at a school that was struggling more than most in the state. I was so excited and optimistic on my first day. Tragically, there was a shooting near the school, and we had to lock down the campus. *On the first day of my dream job!*

Nonetheless, on day two, I knew that if I was going to make the impact that I sought, I'd have to reach a new level of preparation, understanding, and strategy. And that's what I did.

There is a level of preparation that accompanies success in any endeavor. As an assistant principal, I read every book I could find on how to turn a school around. I met with successful principals, I constantly reflected on my impact, and I attended every single school board meeting for two years. I wanted to understand the politics, procedures, and hidden agendas of the school systems. The only way I could ensure that every student enjoyed every class was if I were in a position to have input on every teacher hire. I needed to become a principal. My philosophy would ensure that new teachers would not be hired just to teach, but also to make the subjects relevant for the students by making a real connection between the material and the students' lives.

I was rejected for 10 principal positions in my district, yet I never lost that desire, passion, and commitment. And most importantly, I maintained a positive and growth mindset. Deep down, I knew that all I needed was one "yes." Then, one day, I got a call stating that the superintendent wanted to meet with me at 1 p.m.

I was nervous. Curious if I did something wrong, I entered the superintendent's office at 1 p.m. sharp and left with a new job. I had been offered the principal role at an underperforming junior high school. I would start the very next day.

"I am tired of hearing what students can't do in a building where the teachers run the school," the superintendent said. "They need a principal to show them what students can accomplish with effective leadership."

How about that? I hadn't been an executive principal a day in my life, and the superintendent was already calling me an effective leader. That superintendent was investing in me. He believed in me. He was speaking life into me. He was setting the stage for me to be successful in an improbable situation.

So, at the age of 29, I had a new job. I was the principal of a low-performing junior high school comprised of 979 students with an economically disadvantaged population of 95.4%, and I needed to get the teachers to respect my role. I was fired up. I had so many ideas and expectations, so many things I wanted to try. I knew we could turn the school around. I had been preparing for this moment for years. Or so I thought.

Expectation versus Reality

Whenever anyone enters a new position, they are full of hope, promise, gusto, and vision. The newly hired comes in with a confident attitude that they have what it takes to improve the situation. Yet, with new opportunity comes old theory. For me, the theory was to simply duplicate what had worked on other campuses, the theory of the philosophers who came before me. The newly hired will gravitate toward the theories they have seen work.

I had a goal. My eye was on the prize. Of course, it was not easy. First of all, I was the youngest principal in the district. Second, I replaced the junior high's then principal abruptly, leaving the faculty no time to grieve or process the loss of their leader. Third, I was not prepared to lead this campus. I did not have the data and had no idea what I was walking into. All I knew is that it was the second-lowest performing school in the district at that time.

So, there I came, with my passion and commitment and can-do attitude. I was armed with the traditional ways you turn a school around, because I wanted to do right by the superintendent and succeed. One of my first orders of business was to meet with the teachers individually, garner their insights as to strengths and weaknesses of the campus, and begin to identify trends in data. I had to assess the attributes of the leadership team, and establish procedures and protocols based on the information gathered.

Several weeks into my newly appointed role, I communicated an expectation to the teachers that they should submit the goals portion of their evaluation process by a specific deadline. I was motivated by private communication with the superintendent, who had told me that the culture of our teachers was subpar. I communicated my expectations clearly, or so I thought. Out of over 60 teachers, only four submitted the goals at the appointed time and in the appropriate manner.

These teachers really do whatever they want to do. They have no respect for authority. I am going to hold them accountable, I thought. So, I wrote them up. Well, not really. I handed out pink slips of paper with something along the lines of "my actions were unacceptable," and asked them to sign the paper. My goal was to establish a culture of accountability, but the teachers did not respond well to my request.

What came next can only be described as a war of wits, a tsunami of tasks, and choke hold of change. My feeble attempts to achieve my goal were met with mistrust. I immediately created an "us versus them" culture. They perceived me as acting authoritarian, which had not been my intention. Leaders have a hard enough job as it is. Try leading a group of people who do not trust you and who think you're out to get them.

My teachers thought I didn't value what they had to offer. I received multiple grievances for a variety of things. There were even grievances over our parking lot situation. The long-tenured teachers had parking spots closer to the door of the school, whereas the newer teachers had to park really far from the entrance. I ended the parking lot favoritism and even said, "You can park in my spot if you want. You just have to beat me to it."

It did not go well. Whenever a grievance is filed, there are lawyers, human resource investigations, unions, and all sorts of other groups involved. I spent so much time preparing to deal with each grievance, when I wanted to spend that time "fixing" the school. My reputation was that of a "taskmaster." People quit. We started to see some incremental change throughout the school, but it felt forceful. It wasn't sustainable.

My first year was one of success in many ways, and one of failure as well. The success was my focus on what it takes to move a school instructionally. My failure was my complete lack of awareness of what it takes to inspire others to do things with you and not for you.

How can you be called an effective leader if no one is following you?

Key Points

- The purpose of school is to ensure learning.

- When entering a new opportunity, it is fine to enter with hopes, dreams, and even expectations, but remember the process is just as important as the goal.

- Listen, observe, and understand before assuming you know what is best.

CHAPTER 2 - SUCCESS

"For our success to be real, it must contribute to the success of others."

– Eleanor Roosevelt

Now, I am not going to make you comb through these pages searching for the No. 1 secret to success. Instead, I am going to share it with you right here, right now. No matter what the issues are, be they systemic or funding related or even faculty based, you already have everything you need to ensure transformation of your school. You don't need to invest in a $50K "teach the teachers" course. You do not need fancy gadgets or even to hire a multitude of consultants (which means a lot coming from me since I *am* an educational/leadership consultant). You can develop quality teachers and ensure high-performing students with what you already have available.

That's right. Everything you need is already within you.

Notice I said *ensure* transformation. There is a big difference between doing and ensuring. To do something means to take some sort of action. For our purposes, that action is to improve a situation. To ensure something is to make sure it happens. Ensuring means to guarantee. Doing is activity focused. Ensuring is results focused.

The wise words of John Wooden, one of the most successful basketball coaches in collegiate history, come to mind. "Never mistake activity for achievement." Think about that quote for a moment. There is plenty of activity in education. There is plenty of "doing." But today, we are suffering from a deficiency of student achievement. As leaders, we need to reflect—and, if necessary, shift—our focus to ensure learning and much more.

But first, you have to cast aside everything you know about education and leadership to start with a blank slate.

The Biggest Lesson

There are two things I wish I would have known then that I know now. The first is that I wish I had paid attention to the process more than the goal. Goals are very important. Goals are our vision, our guiding light. However, you have to think through and appreciate the *process*. Leaders get things done with and through people, which brings me to the second thing and biggest lesson of all: I wish I would have known the importance of investing in people.

"Don't spend time on people," I now tell my leaders. The statement usually leaves people with a quizzical glance, so allow me to explain it a bit further: You may have heard the saying "Make your money work for you." The theory behind it is not to "spend time" in order to make money, but to put that money somewhere it can grow. Therefore, instead of spending time on people, *invest* time in people so they become a bigger asset than they were before.

As a young leader, I thought I knew it all. I thought I had the answer. I came into that school so full of what I thought, so focused on the goals and expectations, that I missed sight of the people who could help me. The reality is that you do very little by yourself. You cannot fire your way to success. Principals do not teach the math class or the physics class. It is imperative that you invest in and empower others so that you can work collaboratively in alignment with the vision.

I was trying to fix a school instead of investing in the people. I was taking the hard line of, "We are going to do this, and I don't care what you think about it. This is where we are headed. Get over it." And I was trying to accomplish a task without understanding the people who were integral to its success.

Believe it or not, I stayed at that school for a total of three years. By the third year, we experienced a complete transformation in the culture. I spent the entire second and third year investing in the people. When I left, it was a voluntary departure to take a position in the same district at one of the high schools. By then, we were functioning as an aligned team focused on student learning. As a result, student achievement increased to such a degree that the campus earned three distinctions from the state in the areas of reading, mathematics, and top 25% student progress. A distinction designation acknowledges campuses for outstanding achievement. Distinction designations are based on performance relative to a group of campuses of similar type, size, grade span, and student demographics throughout the state. A campus earns a distinction designation if it is in the top quartile of its comparison group.

Investing in People

Whether you are a new leader assigned to a new school with the hopes of bringing about positive change or a seasoned veteran determined to transform your existing educational landscape, the first things you need to do are to listen, ask, and observe before acting on any issues. Dispel any notion in your mind that you know it all. Believe me, you probably do not.

When you are talking about building relationships with people, you first need to understand where they are and why they are where they are. Ask yourself, *What has this individual experienced that has led them to this belief and to the outcomes they are pursuing?*

I am a firm believer that your experience fosters your beliefs, your beliefs influence your actions, and your actions produce your results. The hardest thing to do is to change a person's belief system as to why they do their job, how they do their job, and what it means to them to do their job.

Reconciling that complexity becomes a problem with leadership, because leaders often deal with people from an action and result standpoint. For example, a principal might say to a teacher, "Try this plan or try this strategy," as an action to get a different result. When you start from there, and you work with people from an action mindset, the relationship is superficial. You are focused on the outcome, not the person. You will have what I had during my first year as principal: compliance, but not commitment. By only focusing on actions and results, you ignore the fact that people think. Guess what? There are reasons why people think the way they do. Therefore, you leave unchanged the two elements that fundamentally affect performance: experience and beliefs.

Instead, put the action mindset aside. Start with the experience. If you can understand where a person is coming from and who they are, you are in a better place to understand what it is going to take to relate to them. You will be in a better position to create more sustainable and significant change, but it also takes more effort. My "rapping history student" is a great example. I did not judge the student. I did not focus on the results first. Instead, I inspected the student experience and observed the behaviors that student enjoyed. I was able to take that observation and build a learning relationship with the student.

All it took was a little time.

For anyone in leadership, I recommend doing what I did with my student: Observe, Listen, and Adapt (OLA). Observe with open eyes, listen to understand, and adapt to what you've learned. You will be hard pressed to find a problem for which OLA will not at least help you to discover a solution.

Indeed, time is the most important factor you have as a leader. Nothing is more valuable. After all, we are only given a finite amount of time throughout our lives, right? Giving someone your undivided attention and time are essential components of investing in people. It demonstrates the value of the interaction. And the act can be as simple as projecting the right body language.

When someone comes to your office, do you stop everything, lock in, and make eye contact? Do you share that time with them no matter how busy you may be? If you do, then you must know that focus conveys a critical message. Your actions silently say: *You know I am busy, but right now you are the most important thing in my life.* That message alone means the world to people, and it is so simple to practice. To be the recipient of someone's time is a respectful gesture and an inspiring feeling.

Say you don't do those things. Maybe you check emails while meeting with someone or find it difficult to focus and maintain eye contact. What does that say? It says, *I do not value this time with you.* It says, *There are other important things going on besides you.* It is a surefire way to uninvest in people.

Such investment tactics get simpler and simpler. Stop and think about the last time you took the time to write a handwritten letter to anyone on your team as a way to celebrate and acknowledge them. I made it a point to write a handwritten note daily to at least one member of my staff for various occasions. It could have been something as simple as "I saw the level of focus you had while grading the other day. Keep up the great work." The notes were meaningful, genuine, and even unexpected. When your actions really show people you care about them, you create an experience for them that cultivates a relationship with people who also appreciate you in return.

We have a lot of leaders who have the title of leader but not the spirit of leadership. The spirit of leadership is about the people. I would have teachers who would not take a day off, who would show up to work every single day. So, I would write handwritten notes to their spouses and children, saying, "I know you needed your mom/dad/partner at home with you, but thank you for being so selfless that you allowed them to come to work each and every day." A note like that has a ripple effect. Now, you are building relationships with the people about whom your teachers care the most.

Acknowledge the sacrifice your team makes each day to show up and do their best. Yes, it is a job. Yes, a paycheck is rewarded once a month or every two weeks. But, just like you, your people live an entire world outside their job.

I gave teachers gift cards, acknowledged them in the school newsletter, and ensured parents were a part of celebrating those teachers with perfect attendance. After all, the entire group was benefitting from those teachers' steadfast dedication, so why wouldn't we celebrate all of them as well? Those steps were fundamental building blocks to a culture of appreciation.

I even went beyond giving them my personal recognition. When I worked at the high school after my three years as principal at the middle school, I started a mission to get President Barack Obama to acknowledge my teachers who had perfect attendance. I wanted to celebrate those teachers at the highest level possible, while also improving teacher attendance.

The first year, I sent one letter and one email to the White House requesting that acknowledgement. I received no response.

Undeterred by the lack of response, I doubled my efforts the next year. We emailed and mailed a letter every day during the last six weeks of the school year, requesting acknowledgment. The letter went as follows:

Dear Mr. President,

There are few professions more honorable than that of the professional educator. Teaching requires more than just dissemination of information; it demands the skill to convey content in a relevant way, combined with the passion to reach the hearts and minds of often unmotivated and distracted students.

Teaching is a demanding and sometimes thankless profession. It can take a toll on both the body and the mind. Teachers who selflessly refuse to use the days that they have been given to be absent so as to ensure that students never miss out on an opportunity to learn from the most qualified asset in the school, their teacher, should be recognized and celebrated. As the Principal, I understand the dedication and commitment that it takes to inspire, motivate, and educate our youth. I am asking you to join me in celebrating my teachers with perfect attendance. Please consider sending an official memorandum in appreciation of their service.

The persistence paid off. The next summer, the White House responded with letters addressed to each teacher with perfect attendance at my campus.

Investing in people is about creating opportunities to show you care. When you are genuine and persistent, relationships are built on a foundation of trust. People start to understand your heart, and you start to understand them as well. When those teachers received a letter from the president congratulating them for perfect attendance, they were so proud. Teacher attendance skyrocketed the following year, and the president wrote us again.

Now, the letters were a really great motivator for our teachers to establish excellent attendance. They were proud, and they were excited. But the investment in people didn't stop with the teachers. Since teachers were consistently showing up each and every day, students were learning. That consistency forged positive relationships between the teachers and their learners. Less time was spent having substitutes fill in lessons with "busywork." Less time was spent trying to make sure classrooms were covered. Students knew that every day they woke up and went to class, their teacher would be there. And that certainty meant something.

Nothing in life comes without being consistent. Consistency develops routines and builds momentum. It forms habits that become almost second nature. When you care about people, you care about what they do and what they experience. The most effective leaders understand that outcome. Robert Joss (2007), former dean of Stanford Graduate School of Business, says:

> The minute you move from being a task-oriented professional to being a leader, it stops being about your individual talents, your successes, and starts being all about coaching, motivating, teaching, supporting, removing roadblocks, and finding resources for your employees. Leadership is about celebrating their victories and rewarding them; helping them analyze when things don't go to plan. Their successes become your successes. Their failures are yours too.

Investing in people is paramount. Your investment in people will encourage them to go to work, while you assist them along the way. On your first day in a leadership role, begin the process of encouraging, shaping, motivating, and developing your people into exceptional examples.

And If You Don't Invest in Others?

What happens if you choose not to invest in others? Well, in my case, the staff filed a myriad of grievances, and people quit left and right. Worse, the culture impeded our ability to ensure student learning. The school's core rested on the shoulders of uncertainty and mistrust. Gossip prevailed. Basically, we discovered cracks in our cultural foundation.

When you invest in others, you keep your promises, no matter how small. You listen and try to understand. You are proactive and do things without being asked. You find genuine, unique, and meaningful ways to celebrate others' progress and goals. Those actions create trust and security.

By investing in others, we are being intentional about managing the perception of others. Misperception can be a base for conflict. If we perceive others as an adversary and act accordingly, we will generate responses in kind.

Effective leadership shapes employee experience, engagement, and well-being, all of which are vital to a thriving workplace culture. The leader sets the tone for what is valued. If the leader values people, then others will as well. When administration values and invests in the staff, then staff will, in turn, value and invest in parents, students, and the community.

As a leader, you need to make people believe they can succeed and show them what you want and expect of them. Philosopher-poet Johann Wolfgang von Goethe advised, "When we treat [people] as if they were what they should be, we improve them as far as they can be improved."

Keys to Ensure Success by Investing in Others

First and foremost, you must focus on the investment, not the return. When you focus on the return, you are focused on what you are up against, not on what you can control. Attitudes, emotions, situations, challenges, and circumstances will always stand in the way of progress. It is important, however, to focus on what you can influence. Had I known that lesson when I started my work as principal, I could have avoided a lot of heartache. But I am so grateful for that experience and everything I learned from it. Remember that the process is just as important as the goal, if not even more important than the goal.

The next key of success is to think *understand,* instead of *understood.* In the book, *7 Habits of Highly Effective People,* true transformative leadership lies in Habit 5: "Seek first to understand, then to be understood." As a school leader, you need to incorporate the time, space, and permission to listen to what teachers are saying without thinking of a response. Stop. Listen. Your teachers are on the ground. They are the ears, eyes, and heart of the school. Unless you can purposefully seek to understand others' perspectives, you could risk misinterpreting ripples in your school's culture as "other people's problems," when those ripples could, in fact, be a leadership problem.

Finally, commit to the high road. Clearly, people let us down on occasion—sometimes in a way that sends shock waves through our system due to someone's complete inability to exhibit any level of self-awareness or appreciation for all the things you, your team, and your organization have done for that person. Oftentimes, those people who have been given the most are the ones who appreciate it the least. When such instances inevitably happen, remember it is not your fault. Your efforts are not pointless. Do not second-guess yourself for a moment. Take the high road. You will get all your efforts back in different ways, with different people.

Once you've embraced the notion of investing in others, it is time to inspect the very ways you can ensure learning with your students.

Reflective Activity 2.1: "Investment"

When it comes to reflecting on your investment in others, consider asking the following questions:

Reflective Questions:

1. Am I engaged more in spending time with or investing time in others?

2. In what ways can I improve my investments in others?

3. What challenges or barriers would hinder my improvement?

4. How do I plan to overcome those barriers or challenges to ensure quality investment in others?

5. Identify three things you want people to remember about your leadership.

Key Points

- Acknowledge the sacrifice your team makes each day to show up and do their best.

- Effective leadership shapes employee experience, engagement, and well-being.

- Seek first to understand and then to be understood.

- The difference between doing and ensuring comes down to *guaranteeing* something is getting done versus simply getting something done.

- Don't spend time on people; invest time in people.

- The simplest gestures are sometimes the most influential.

CHAPTER 3 - EMPOWER LEARNERS

"Children are likely to live up to what you believe of them."

– Lady Bird Johnson

As we journey through this chapter, I'd like to remind you of this idea: The purpose of school is not just to teach. The purpose of school is to ensure learning. We are going to discuss what it means to ensure that your teachers are successful facilitators of a classroom of learners. That triumph is paramount to ensuring clarity of the mission. What does such success even look like?

First, let's explore what we mean by the phrase "ensure learning." There are a few acceptable definitions of the concept, but in short, it means that the teacher has determined what constitutes as acceptable evidence of comprehension in the outcomes and/or results (assessment). I often use a tactic to ensure clarity. I ask to whomever I am speaking, "What did you take from this conversation?" They will assuredly respond with what was most important to them in that moment. Ensuring learning follows the same concept. It is teaching the material in a way that meets all students' learning styles. When assessed for competency and comprehension, students are able to provide evidence of their understanding—the *learning*—at the level it was intended.

Ensuring learning also means the instructional leader has established the systems and processes to verify that expectations are being met. There has to be continuity.

Consistency, or the absence of it, can be the defining factor between failure or success. Effective educational leaders should always develop a consistent and established mission to make the process of learning and the student experience a priority.

When you have a student (or even students) who do not find the instructional content worthy of their time or effort, a few questions will arise. Students will ask themselves or their teacher: (1) How is this information going to benefit me? and (2) What does this information have to do with me?

Those questions should not be dismissed as an act of insubordination or disruption. The students are simply seeking relevance. Think about your own experience as a student. Was there a subject where you thought to yourself, *When will I ever need to know this in real life?* It is human nature to question relevancy, but our goal as educational leaders is to eliminate the need for that question.

Relevance

While it may be true that many educators often undervalue the importance of relevance as an aspect of teaching and learning, we know from research that teaching without relevance can be demotivating to students. Students who are demotivated find other things to capture their attention, and those things might be destructive. It should be refreshing then to realize that inattentive, unmotivated behaviors could simply be due to a lack of relevance in what is being taught. Why? Because that problem has a myriad of solutions.

Relevancy can easily be established by showing how the lesson can be applied in practice, establishing relevance to local cases, relating material to everyday applications, or finding applications in current newsworthy issues. Students deserve relevant and interesting lessons that also match their individual learning styles.

Take geometry. A student may question the relevance of the Pythagorean theorem. In what ways can a teacher establish relevance? Perhaps they can apply the theorem to a construction project involving angles. Or they could use a video game to illustrate the concept. The key is to find out what is most relevant to students and build the lesson around that relevance.

What about finding relevance in history? We all know that history often repeats itself. Are there historical concepts that contain similarities with current events? The events that hold the most significance for any given person are typically those events that occur in the present. Teachers can help bridge the past to the present for students by developing a scavenger hunt. Can students spot the similarities and differences between a historical and present-day event? Once students establish correlations for themselves and discover historical and present-day connections, they can begin to uncover the relevance of their history lesson. Students deserve to recognize when they have learned something and feel a sense of accomplishment. As students recognize their own learning, their sense of pride and hunger for additional learning increases. But elevating those outcomes into reality all begins with the teacher and his or her perceptions.

Such focus and follow-through can be taught and learned. As a principal, I would often challenge interviewees by telling them, "I'm not hiring you to focus exclusively on your teaching." They would often look at me, eyes wide, and maybe crack a smile of uncertainty. I'd quickly follow it up with, "I'm hiring you to ensure students learn."

Oftentimes, I would get a nod indicating a hint of understanding, but due to the weight, complexity, and ambiguousness of my statement, I had to ensure clarity. I would then ask them, "What does that mean to you?"

A Room Full of Students versus a Room Full of Learners

Perception shapes, defines, and influences the experience of our personal reality. We believe that what we perceive to be reality is accurate. With that perception, we create our own realities. A plethora of research has been completed on how teacher perceptions shape student experiences, for better or for worse. Of the most notable is research on the Pygmalion Effect, also known as the self-fulfilling prophecy.

In their research, Rosenthal and Jacobsen (1968) demonstrated how teacher expectations influence student performance, both positively and negatively. When teachers have positive expectations, they influence student performance positively. Ditto for negative expectations. That reinforcing cycle is where beliefs shape expectations. Because expectations shape actions and behaviors, those actions and behaviors affect outcomes for better and for worse. Effective leaders work to ensure a healthy, positive, unbiased, and inclusive perspective of all learners.

If a teacher perceives his or her classroom to be a room full of students, ensuring the highest degree of success in student achievement will be a challenge. You see, the word "student" connotes compliance and an external form. Perceiving a classroom of students places the teacher in a purely authoritarian role instead of a collaborative one. The teacher tells the students what to read and what information to retain. The teacher assigns, instructs, and supervises, and the students are expected to obey and comply.

What guides those instructions? Is it standards set by the district? Is it benchmarks for passing and failing? Are those lessons hidden in a binder somewhere? Are they expected to be universally taught?

Effective leaders support, encourage, and inspire teachers to rethink their perspective of the classroom. They help teachers take ownership of their individual approaches to teaching. Effective leaders help teachers transform their perspectives from a "room full of students" to something entirely active and collaborative: a room full of learners.

By approaching their classrooms as rooms full of learners, teachers aren't simply teaching; they are guiding. They are preparing for a collaborative experience, not an authoritarian approach. Teachers are showing up to ensure learning, not to ensure teaching. Being a learner implies a limitless opportunity to obtain knowledge. Meanwhile, being a student implies being taught a limited amount of knowledge. Can you see the difference?

Learners ask questions, find answers, think critically, and work together. Learners are driven by their curiosity to never stop seeking (and owning) and developing abilities. That open investigation of knowledge also enables learners to discover their strengths and social-emotional needs without feeling slowed down by traditional educational constraints.

By being encouraged to explore possibilities, learners can meet new ideas and areas of interest, rather than simply finding an answer to a particular question or regurgitating knowledge in the form of a test. That desire will aid learners later in their careers when they can arrive at unusual solutions to ordinary problems.

Teaching and "seeing" learners, instead of just students, implies that education is no longer just a one-way path with the teacher as a lecturer and deliverer of knowledge. Teachers become *facilitators* who work together with learners to accomplish results. Those they teach are encouraged to take ownership of their learning. That approach especially makes sense when we think about the pace of change rapidly evolving today. Teachers cannot be a source of all knowledge and distribute access to information while simultaneously providing opportunities for the learner to collaborate with them.

Team effort is required. It prepares learners to work with others and across functional areas, which will be expected of them in the future. By learning that the work that's being done is valuable beyond their own gained knowledge, learners feel a greater purpose. They will begin to think about how their co-creation of knowledge can benefit others with different skill sets. Collaboration fosters a sense of limitless possibility and solidifies a sense of relevance within the learners' lives. Simply by developing an appreciation for shared input, learners are more likely to welcome many different points of view.

Let's say you have a teacher who enters the classroom, sees a room full of students, and starts rattling off the rules. He or she shares the syllabus and tells the students, "This is what we're learning this year." Then, he or she dives into page one of chapter one of the textbook and asks the first student in the first row to read the first page out loud. Now, that example is very harsh, but if a teacher establishes a rapport of "This is what I'm teaching, and you will learn it this way," the odds of successfully ensuring learning begin to dwindle.

What if that teacher enters school on the first day and sees a room full of learners? Together the class makes the rules, and the teacher adds a few expectations. He or she then shares the syllabus, but tells the students, "There might be some things not on here that you are curious about, and I'll make sure we explore those topics as well." Then, instead of cracking open the book, he or she establishes a baseline for what the learners might know about the particular topic in a friendly, open discussion, or fun exercise.

Which classroom is going to be more successful in ensuring learning? Which classroom is more collaborative? Substituting learners for students is an exciting opportunity for all parties. The change in perspective provides a challenge for educators because the fact is learners can learn without us.

For many leaders, shifts in thinking like moving from seeing students to seeing learners is challenging, but often leaders say they are ready for the change. However, you can't just *say* that you want change; you must actually have a motivational desire to make it happen. Ask yourself questions that start with *what, when, where, how,* and *who,* with respect to your desire for change. Avoid asking *why* questions because the answers to those are judgment calls that will prevent objective progress. Examples of good questions include: "When do my beliefs contradict my actions?" "Who is affected by my beliefs?" And "What would it be like to think the opposite of my belief?" In asking such questions, your brain will yield answers that reveal the true nature of your underlying belief. Keep asking questions until you uncover the core belief that is driving you.

Then, identify potentially damaging consequences of holding onto the belief. For example, holding onto the belief that others are incapable of accomplishing success prevents you from challenging and supporting them in their pursuit of achievements.

Next, if you need to modify your belief, you must not only identify your new belief but incorporate it into daily practice. That transition may not be easy. Depending on how long you have lived and breathed your old belief, you may have an emotional bond with it. If you truly want to change, you will need to have the strength and courage to undergo a change in thinking.

Start by implementing methods that support your new belief. Conditioning yourself to your new belief means creating the reality that you want for yourself in your mind and visualizing the results you want to achieve. Begin to visualize a well-behaved, respectful, orderly, highly successful class of learners. Visualization is a great way to create anticipation and concrete results.

Independent versus Dependent Learners

There are two types of learners in every classroom, and educators take the brunt of responsibility for fostering each.

The first type consists of *independent learners*. They are the students who can function with very little direction and equally little feedback. They catch on quickly, and if they don't know the answer, they follow their curiosity and seek out resources on their own. Independent learners feel encouraged and safe to do so. These learners typically interpret instruction in a way that provides them opportunities to think critically, engage in regular self-assessments, and reflect on their learning: "How am I learning? What do I need to work on next? How should I approach this new task?" Their curiosity is rewarded, and their learning is easily ensured.

The second type is composed of *dependent learners*. In their case, the teacher owns the entire learning process. In fact, some dependent learners don't even know if they are learning or not. Dependent learners show up to school each day and sit passively, awaiting instruction. They require feedback to keep them progressing. They typically receive instruction based on test taking and memorization of facts.

That approach is somewhat akin to saying, "Here! Don't worry about thinking too much about it. Just memorize this!" While there is nothing inherently wrong with dependent learners, the goal is to enable all learners to become more independent. Conversion invites collaboration wherein the learner is also taking ownership of the learning process. Helping students understand where they are in the learning process and where they are going is what enables them to grow. That progress is far more important than "getting it right." Together, the teacher and learner can achieve great things.

Instruction enabling both dependent and independent learners is prevalent in education. It's no wonder low-performing kids simply give up. Instead of helping students accelerate their learning to catch up to their grade-level peers, "support" classes often make students get further and further behind.

An unintended consequence of these "support" classes is making those students more and more dependent. Dependent learners need teachers' time and guidance the most in order to become independent learners.

On the flip side, the skills needed for independent thinking are at the forefront of learning how to be a great thinker and a great leader. Such skills teach our learners how to make sense of the world based on personal experience and observation. It encourages them to make critical, well-informed decisions in the same way. Accordingly, they gain confidence and the ability to learn from mistakes as they build successful and productive lives.

Lead the Learner

Effective leaders need to be able to answer two fundamental questions: (1) How do you know if students are learning? (2) When they are not, what do you do about it?

To ensure that every classroom is occupied by independent learners, both perceived and in reality, effective leaders take the time to walk the campus and monitor how well teachers' beliefs align with their actions to inspire, motivate, encourage, and ensure student success. The effective leader must ensure that each teacher develops a learning environment relevant to and reflective of their students' social, cultural, and linguistic experiences. Teachers act as guides, mediators, consultants, instructors, and advocates for their students, helping to effectively connect their culturally and community-based knowledge to the classroom learning experiences.

Taking Action

No matter what you do in your life, if you are going to transform something, you have to engage with it. You cannot change what you avoid.

When it becomes apparent that teacher beliefs are misaligned with the culture and climate of the educational organization, what do you do about it? Unfortunately, most leaders avoid addressing negative attitudes, which means that unchecked beliefs, and sometimes even actions, will have a compounding effect on student achievement. Fear of union interference, fear of conflict, and/or a lack of confidence in bucking tradition are just several of the many reasons for such avoidance. Ignoring actions and attitudes that are detrimental to student achievement is tantamount to child abuse. Students deserve better!

Leaders who are unwilling to confront incompetence or a lack of commitment to the school's mission—among even a few faculty members—will pay the price in the following ways:

- Teacher morale will decrease.

- Behavioral problems will increase.

- Academic achievement will decrease.

- Trust and respect from parents and students for you and the school will decrease.

- The school's effective teachers will feel devalued and less empowered.

The secret to working through value conflicts among teachers is to find the sweet spot where people can understand and respect why others hold certain values, even if they don't agree with them. It is a commitment to seeking first to understand before seeking to be understood. Then, you can create a work environment that leverages the values you do share, such as integrity, honesty, and civility. To do it effectively, you must first commit to being a *character builder.* That commitment means serving as a role model whose values, words, and deeds are marked by trustworthiness, integrity, authenticity, respect, generosity, and humility. An effective leader is an effective communicator. Be genuine and open with the capacity to listen, empathize, interact, and connect with teachers in productive, helping, and healing ways. An effective leader should communicate expectations, offer support, suggest options, and provide instructional resources. Ultimately, effective leaders commit to enlightening teachers of roadblocks and behaviors that impede productivity in the classroom and the achievement of your school-wide mission.

In her book *Fierce Conversations*, Susan Scott defines a fierce conversation as "one in which we come out from behind ourselves into the conversation and make it real." Often, when leaders meet with difficult teachers, they end up talking too much and saying all the wrong things. They ask inane questions or sugarcoat the discussion with ill-advised compliments to avoid hurting teachers' feelings. They often don't get to the point or tell the truth. They babble and dance around the elephant in the room. Dealing with dysfunctional teachers requires character, assertiveness, communication skills, a servant's heart, and the courage to confront inappropriate behavior the first time it becomes evident. As an effective leader, it is your responsibility to address teachers in your building who have a mindset focused only on teaching instead of on ensuring that students learn.

Key Points

- Schools are institutions of learning, not just teaching.

- To ensure learning, teachers must ensure clarity in the classroom.

- Students crave relevancy of lessons to their everyday lives.

- Teachers need to shift their perspective and see a classroom full of learners instead of a classroom full of students.

- An effective leader is an effective communicator.

CHAPTER 4 - LEARNING AND QUALITY INSTRUCTION

"The most common cause of failure in leadership is produced
by treating adaptive challenges as if they were technical problems."

– Ron Heifetz

Shifting from a focus on ensuring learners, we now turn our attention to ensuring learning. After all, we do not hire teachers only to teach, but also to ensure students are learning. But how do we ensure learning? Are grades not the perfect benchmarks for evidence of learning? (Spoiler alert: They are only part of the evidence equation.) First, we must examine the equation of evidence as a whole.

The Outcomes and Assessments for Ensuring Learning

Effective teachers must find ways to monitor evidence of competency and comprehension among their learners. There must be a strategic system and process (or culmination of systems and processes) for evaluation.

Pause for a moment and consider this: What does a grade tell you? It is a numeric value assigned to a project, paper, test, or participation benchmark. Does it assess learning? Does a grade ensure learning?

Grades are meant to evaluate learning and performance; however, grades are sometimes treated as a proxy for student learning. Perhaps the invention of grades was meant to assess student learning, but since education has evolved over the years, grades are not always a reliable measure of what a student knows or understands. In fact, grades cannot even adequately assess a student's cognitive level.

We see that disconnect when teachers give grades that, on paper, show a classroom performing at a high level while students' scores on district or state assessments don't always correlate to that classroom-wide high performance. That disparity isn't to say the teacher is lying or that the learners suddenly forgot all the information that they were taught throughout the year. The difference just means that sometimes grades are not truly an assessment of learning.

Indeed, effective instructional leaders embrace and understand eight misconceptions about grades and assessments.

MISCONCEPTION #1 – ASSESSMENT AND EVALUATION ARE THE SAME EXACT THING

Unfortunately, many educators, particularly those at the secondary level, continue to cling tenaciously to the traditional practices, which are counterproductive to the goals of modern education. All too often, we evaluate student work and tell ourselves that what we have done is an assessment.

Assessment involves giving timely, detailed feedback based around clearly defined learning outcomes. Simply stated, the teacher has ensured clarity around those learning outcomes, and the assessment is feedback based. Assessments are not pass/fail. Rather, they are strength/improvement based. Assessments are timely. You can't have an honest dialogue with a learner while only assessing learning outcomes from the beginning of the quarter to the end of the quarter.

Evaluation is giving a grade to a piece of work, usually based on normative criteria. If the whole class doesn't do well, teachers might be motivated to instill a grading curve, thus benchmarking evaluation on the student with the highest evaluation. That option is not a true assessment of learning. Both processes can be formative (undertaken while an educational process is ongoing) or summative (taken at the conclusion of an educational process).

Rule for success: It is crucial to communicate to everyone whether you are conducting an assessment or an evaluation.

MISCONCEPTION #2 – DATA INFORMS BEST DECISIONS

Data is good; information is better. Data and information are similar concepts, but they are not the same thing. Data is a part, a segment, a snippet. Information is the whole. If I tell you that you are at the 80th percentile, or scored in the 4th quintile, or had a RIT score of 280, would you be able to decide what to do next? Why do leaders trust that district and state decisions based on data are more relevant than teacher's insights and information?

Assessment that is relevant, mutual, engaging, and instructive leads to student success. Data informs some decisions, but information is much more comprehensive.

Rule for success: To ensure the right decision, ask yourself, *How am I converting data to information to better understand the reason for the differences in results?* Also ask yourself, *How am I using the information to make better decisions when addressing challenges?*

MISCONCEPTION #3 – MOST ASSESSMENTS ARE SUMMATIVE

Along the lines of timely feedback, many teachers wrongfully assume assessments are summative, meaning the focus is on the outcome of a specific program or class. We need to continually assess both student work and the quality of teaching throughout the semester. By the time we get to the end of a unit or the end of a lesson, learners should have had multiple opportunities to rethink and redo their work. Learning is the journey, not the destination. After we finish a journey, we often assess ourselves at the end of it. One summative assessment will not measure learning.

Remember, learners can learn as much from teachers as those teachers can learn from their learners. (That fact will bring us to our next misconception.)

Rule for success: Establish assessment checkpoints along the way.

MISCONCEPTION #4 – ASSESSMENTS ARE A ONE-WAY COMMUNICATION

It is a common misconception that the teacher gives feedback on the learner's work. In traditional assessments and evaluation models, the learner completes a task. Then the teacher assesses the work and tells the learner how they did and what they could have done to improve. A better approach is if a learner engages with their teacher to discuss the work, collaborate through their learning journey, or even explain their rationale, because amazing results can happen. A dialogue forms between the learner and teacher. The teacher gains more insight into how the learner learns. The learner gains insight on what the teacher is hoping to ensure. Both parties benefit from the experience.

Rule for success: Establish opportunities for students to dialogue about their learning.

MISCONCEPTION #5 – ASSESSMENTS ARE FOR GRADING PURPOSES

Traditionally, an assessment earned a grade in the classroom. That custom is the most pervasive and damaging holdover from traditional teaching. Yes, grades should reflect what has gone on between the learner and the teacher. Grades are necessary! But grades are not tally marks you collect to arrive at a final grade.

Take homework, for example. Homework reinforces a lesson and gives learners the opportunity to practice the concepts that are taught and shared in the classroom. Then, students are graded on their homework, which means that they are graded on their practice.

If you witness a basketball team or a football team practice, often the scoreboard will not display the score as it would in a real game. Practice is designed to help build the skills necessary to compete. It is a time to build each skill set that is important for a sport or any type of competitive performance.

For example, a quarterback needs to break down the mechanics of a pass. He needs to know how to grip the football, how to position his final drop back–plant step, and how to lean his torso forward with his shoulders turned perpendicular to the passing target.

The purpose of practice is to figure out how to correct any mistakes. It is how you grow and get better and stronger. You get the opportunity to think about what you are doing, not doing, or what you need to do differently.

Why should homework be any different? Why should we be grading learners on their practice, on their work that has been done before they have mastered the material?

When a learner sees a failing grade, it damages their confidence. They feel they're not smart, not good enough, and as if their efforts are pointless. They feel as if they are falling behind and that school is not a good investment of their time. Such an effect is not to say that teachers can never give a student an *F* if that is what the student earned, but remember that assessment is not the grade.

In a sense, grading is one by-product of assessment. Teachers assign each student a grade periodically throughout the year to reflect all of a student's performance up to that point in one collective sum. It is not a simple task! But the task should be to construct a grading system that best reflects learning in a way by which students are informed and made aware. Students should know where their grade is coming from. They should know what is valued and should have ways to participate in the process.

Rule for success: Allow for mistakes in the learning process, and provide quality and timely feedback.

MISCONCEPTION #6 – EVERYTHING A LEARNER DOES NEEDS A GRADE

In summative situations where grades are necessary, that practice may be true. Yet, too often, teachers put a grade on everything, hoping to use the work formatively. Learners are graded on participation, homework completion, tests, attendance, projects, teamwork, and the list goes on. As soon as a learner sees a grade on a piece of work, he or she is going to think the learning is done. Got a *C*? Well, then that's as good as it is going to get. That impression couldn't be further from the truth. No matter what the teacher's intention, grades imply a finality. That inference further contributes to a dependent-learner mentality, so be very judicious about what you assign a grade to and what you do not.

Rule for success: Value the learning by providing quality feedback rather than a grade.

MISCONCEPTION #7 – GRADES AND TEST SCORES MAXIMIZE STUDENT MOTIVATION AND LEARNING

A teacher's demands, grades, and promises of additional opportunities are entirely external rewards. Decades of research, both about educational best practices and the way the human mind works, suggests that those types of motivators are dangerous. Offering students rewards for learning will create reliance on the reward, even a fixation. Students will strive for the best grade but only to achieve that letter or number, not to learn the material. Then, if the reward becomes less interesting to the student or disappears entirely, the student's motivation will do the same.

Inspiring students' intrinsic motivation to learn is a more effective strategy to get and keep students interested. And it's more than that. Students actually learn better when motivated that way. They put forth more effort, tackle more challenging tasks, and end up gaining a more profound understanding of the concepts they study. They take ownership of their learning because they are the source of their own motivation.

Rule for success: Frame learning as the reward by asking, "What were you excited to learn about today?"

MISCONCEPTION #8 – AN ASSIGNMENT TURNED IN LATE SHOULD NOT COUNT FOR FULL CREDIT

Decisions are always met with consequences, but consider this: If the focus is truly on learning and ensuring learning, does it matter if a learner turns in an assignment a few days late? Yes, life is full of deadlines, and turning in your rent late or your project to your boss late will come with consequences, but teachers are in the business of ensuring learning, right? If the teacher says everyone is expected to learn material by Monday, and the learner demonstrates learning by Wednesday instead, they are penalized because they have not learned the material in the time the teacher has dictated.

There is nothing wrong with having a consequence for late work, but the assignment of grades should always reflect the learner's learning. If a learner hands in work worthy of an *A* today, is the worth of that work different if it is handed in tomorrow? Why is it now worth a *B*? When teachers rethink and reform their views on what assessments are all about, they can see how assessments properly done can ensure learning and how grading haphazardly impedes learning.

Too often, teachers grade kids on what they do, not what they learn. Grades assess what kids are doing instead of what they are learning. It is like measuring how well kids can borrow information and return it. We don't want our learners to borrow information. We want our learners to buy information. Teachers want buy-in. If you have any doubts, ask any one of your students what they learned in class on a given day. I bet they will tell you what they did, not what they learned.

For example, let's say you asked your student, Sasha, what she learned during yesterday's Geography class.

"We went over the map of Europe and talked about the different countries that make up the European Union," Sasha replies.

Sasha is correct. That is exactly what she did. But what did Sasha learn? Education is so focused on teaching, learning feels secondary. But learning isn't an activity. Learning *is the result* of an activity.

Teachers need to ask the question, "What type of experience do I need to create to allow my learners to demonstrate what they're absorbing?" Teachers need to know what stages it will take to get learners to that learning experience and close the learning gaps. Effective educators cannot understand at what stage the learner is without understanding the person who is learning. We all have different styles of learning. If you don't understand, you can't assess learning. That knowledge is hard to obtain with a huge class, but is why so many educators and educational institutions are struggling.

We've done a lot of damage to kids because we have diminished creative expression and innovative thinking. We have made students dependent on how we want them to do things. Then, thinking our kids have "done" something, we assume they have learned it. That assumption is why there is such a discrepancy between what a teacher says a student has learned and the true amount of learning shown by a student at the end of the year.

Teachers who ask learners, "What do you need from me?" are opening the door for collaboration.

We have to be very clear to talk about what that learning will look like. We have to show it to them. We have to create it for them. We have to help them through the process. And when we give a grade, it is not representative of action or activity; it is representative of learning.

Effective leaders who allow teachers the freedom to use assessments in more productive ways make those assessments more fruitful, meaningful, and far less about the notion of grading.

Avoid shortcuts whenever possible. When it comes to ensuring learning, there are some things that should be nonnegotiable but have become negotiable because of time, other focus, other priorities, and other distractions. Examples of these shortcuts could include a lack of ensuring lessons or assessments are on grade level, misalignment of the "verb" being taught or assessed in relation to the expected standard, and neglecting to have students demonstrate proficiency in the manner in which they will be assessed at the state level. For schools to be truly educational institutions of learning, then everything we do should be focused on the impact of learning.

Rule for success: Ask yourself, *How did I have students demonstrate their learning in order to prove their mastery?*

A Tale of Two Mindsets

My hope is that, by now, your perceptions have shifted slightly after diving into this chapter. There is another key component that will aid in your quest to ensure learning and quality instruction: mindset.

In her book *Mindset*, Stanford University psychologist Carol S. Dweck, Ph.D., outlines how success in school, work, sports, the arts, and almost every area of human achievement can be dramatically influenced by how we perceive our talents and abilities. In education, we endeavor to work with individuals in such a way that we both exemplify and support improvement in mindset. But there are two types of mindset we encounter.

The first type is those who have a *fixed mindset*.

Individuals in that category are less likely to embrace change. They feel that whatever skills they have are all they will have. They are less likely to be flexible as well, always clinging to the status quo. A fixed mindset is a performance-focused mindset. Such individuals may even ask, "How will this situation make me look?" Challenges are roadblocks. Feedback is taken personally. Individuals with a fixed mindset hate making mistakes because they think that making a mistake is a poor reflection on them. A fixed mindset person who looks in a mirror when standing in the midst of a group sees only themselves.

As teachers, they rarely take risks. They play it safe in and out of the classroom. They may even have a passive-aggressive attitude with an air of "it is what it is." They're defeated before they put their lunch in the breakroom fridge.

Students with a fixed mindset feel like they're never going to learn. They have given up before they've entered your classroom. They have allowed a self-fulfilling prophecy to dictate their lives and future ambition. "Well, I'm not good at math," one might say, and they will believe that statement to their core. They will believe it so hard that they will do anything to make it true, even without meaning to do so. It is almost as if they've put up blockers, preventing learning from happening, thanks to their fixed mindset.

We must strive for everyone to develop and embrace a *growth mindset.*

Those with a growth mindset seize opportunities and recognize the transformational power of change. They are the individuals who feel that skills and intelligence can grow and develop over time. A growth mindset is always focused on process and improvement. Challenges are learning opportunities. Individuals who possess a growth mindset love and use feedback for the greater good. Such individuals look in a mirror and see everyone standing behind him or her before noticing their own reflection.

Teachers in that category are flexible and understand he or she may learn from their learners. A growth mindset in a teacher makes them willing to try new things, such as making a mixtape of the Constitution as a rap, or using references to the video game *Fortnite* in math class. These are the teachers who take feedback to heart, but not on the defensive. They use that feedback to improve, to grow, to learn, and to be even better and more effective.

What does a growth mindset look like in students? Well, they aren't afraid to fail. He or she will ask questions and try different ways of learning and growing. Such students trust their instructor and feel safe to ask questions related to their individual learning. There are no self-fulfilling prophecies holding them back.

Based on the two descriptions alone, it is clear which mindset is more effective, desirable, and powerful for educational leaders and teachers alike. Yet, adopting such a mindset is not unmet with challenges.

Two Types of Challenges

We also have two different types of challenges that educational leaders and teachers face every day. They are technical challenges and adaptive challenges.

Technical challenges are problems that are easy to identify. They are easy to solve with existing resources. Technical challenges in education are related to data, strategies, interventions, pacing, and activities, just to name a few. They typically can be solved swiftly by an expert or authority.

Adaptive challenges are, by nature, adaptive. Their definition also means they are fluid and change with circumstances. Adaptive challenges are unpredictable, volatile, complex. They may be hard to identify, but they are easy to deny. The difficulty with those types of challenges is that their solutions usually require people to learn new ways of doing things, change their attitudes, values, and norms, and adopt an experimental mindset. Adaptive challenges deal with relationships, emotional intelligence, empathy, culture, inspiration, and self-awareness. Most importantly, adaptive challenges have to be solved by the people with the problem. You can't call in a quick fix expert to solve an adaptive challenge. In fact, adaptive challenges require constant experimentation.

This is where the growth mindset provides more value, beyond just ensuring learning. It can also tackle both technological and adaptive problems head on.

Technical Solutions for Adaptive Challenges

When you're dealing with people, emotions, relationships, cultures, expectations, and personalities, you are going to encounter adaptive challenges. Is a school made up of these things? Absolutely, which is why for years, traditionally, we have tried to implement technical solutions to adaptive challenges in everything we do in education. Why is that the case?

Well, leaders are always on a timeline. Technical problems are easy to identify. Sometimes, we feel we need to check the boxes. An expert can surely solve the problem, right? Although such excuses are valid, they will prevent all the key players in educational institutions from ensuring learning in the long run. It is like putting a Band-Aid on a gaping wound that requires 50 stitches. It is simply not sustainable.

In education, what type of mindset are we cultivating? When teachers meet, they talk about data, alignment of the curriculum, pacing of lessons, etc. Simply put, teachers and leaders spend a lot of time talking and thinking about technical challenges. Why is that problematic? Well, what you feed grows, what you focus on becomes a priority, and what you monitor becomes a cultural norm. So, if all the focus is on technical solutions to seemingly adaptive challenges, then adaptive challenges will not be addressed and will continue to grow, as will the mindset that nearly all problems in education are technical. The idea couldn't be further from the truth.

An educational leader stands up in front of a teacher-development meeting and says, "We're going to discuss how to ensure learning and unleash the potential of our students today." Then she proceeds to talk about data and pacing and interventions. Someone brings up lesson-planning hacks. Another teacher tells a story about strategies she uses for behavior management. Although ensuring alignment and best practice in each of those areas is vital, they are often discussed in isolation of their impact on student learning. What about the relationships? What about the empowerment of students? What about creating a culture of learning? What about teacher/student empathy? Where do those aspects fall in the meeting? They don't. But they should because they're adaptive challenges. They are what is called the art of teaching.

What we're struggling with the most in education is not data, alignment, or pacing. It is that students are not inspired to learn. Across the country, we are lacking a culture where students are excited about the learning. We're struggling with teachers and students believing they can achieve greatness.

We're struggling with a lack of relationships between students and their classrooms. No data plan or activity assessment is going to solve those problems.

When we cultivate an awareness of adaptive challenges, learning can take place. We can spend all day on technical aspects, but if kids aren't inspired and there is no motivation for them to learn, learning will not be ensured.

Reflective Activity 4.1: "Technical versus Adaptive Challenges"

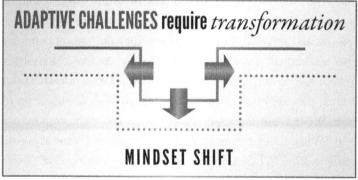

Heifetz, R. and Laurie, D. The work of leadership. Harvard Business Review, Dec. 2001.

Feedback

Feedback is one of the most powerful influences on learning and achievement—if you get it right. It is no secret that feedback should be actionable, timely, and related to agreed-upon learning outcomes. In his book *Visible Learning: Feedback*, John Hattie digs into what research suggests teachers—and administrators—can do to create a culture where adults and students encourage each other to keep learning. Too often feedback is provided that supports the old notion that "only a good teacher is a busy teacher." That premise can't be correct.

A good teacher is one who is prepared to have a discussion about the impact of teaching on student learning. The key question is: does feedback help someone understand what they don't know, what they do know, and where they go to from there? Asking those questions is when and why feedback is so powerful, but a lot of feedback does not help someone understand the answers. Therefore, the feedback does not have any effect.

The popular walk–through model, where the administrator unobtrusively visits the classroom for 2-15 minutes and then provides written or oral feedback on "look-fors" is an inefficient feedback method. It does little to ensure a growth-minded culture to support teacher development and ensure student learning. Such advice doesn't provide true attention and time, which must be taken to engage with teachers regarding the feedback in an intentional and purposeful manner.

Although it might feel counterintuitive to administrators, the first thing they should say during an in-person debriefing session is *nothing*. Full attention should be given to the teacher as you listen. Then, instead of offering advice, the first words out of your mouth should be a question to which you do not know the answer. Only interrupt in order to keep the discussion focused on student learning—for example, When did deep learning occur? What evidence leads you to that conclusion?

Unfortunately, most feedback provided to teachers is relegated to a one-way written analysis, usually prescriptive or descriptive in nature. That method lacks follow-up or a reflective question that probes the teacher to think about evidence of student learning. Prescriptive feedback provides specific directions about what to do differently. Descriptive feedback narrates the teaching performance in detail, including what did and didn't work. Although there is value in both types of feedback, a steady diet of advice and narration leads to an unhealthy inability to reflect, problem-solve, and make new connections and insights.

Lead the Learning

Curious as to the impact of the feedback from administrators to their teachers, I conducted an analysis of feedback across multiple districts, including more than 100 administrators. In each district, it is expected for administrators to conduct walk-throughs on each of their teachers and provide feedback. I collected the feedback and completed a comprehensive analysis. To categorize the feedback that teachers received, I developed a quadrant of four categories: technical teaching, technical learning, adaptive teaching, and adaptive learning, as shown below (or here).

	TECHNICAL	**ADAPTIVE**
TEACHING	Strategies Activities Alignment Engagement Classroom Management Assessments Procedures Planning Pacing	*Reflect on Pedagogy* *Belief in Self* *Establish Culture* *Learning* *Environment*
LEARNING	*Progressive Learning* *Tracking Learning* *Monitoring Learning* *Evidence of Learning*	Feel about Learning Inspired to Learn Empowered to Learn Motivated to Learn Belief about Learning Encouraged to Learn Understanding of the Learning

Technical Teaching

We now know that technical challenges are those that require a quick fix and the involvement of an expert or authority. They are also easily identified. Along the same lines, technical-teaching feedback is categorized as anything that is related to teaching strategies, activities, curriculum alignment, classroom management, procedures, planning, and lesson pacing. Those elements are the areas that hinder a teacher's ability to provide quality, efficient, and/or aligned instruction. The absence or ineffectiveness of such practices contributes to a continual impediment of student progress; however, such feedback is focused on technical aspects of teacher actions and outcomes, and offers no reflective opportunities on student learning.

Example 1

Example of Feedback	Feedback Quadrant	Rationale
How will the goals for learning be communicated to students?	Technical Teaching	The focus of this reflective question is on "goals" and how they will be communicated to students. Goals are technical, and the action of communicating the goals to students is a teacher action. Although the word "learning" appears in this question, there is no actual focus on the teacher's providing evidence of student learning or even reflecting on student learning.

Example 2

Example of Feedback	Feedback Quadrant	Rationale
How do you provide differentiated instructional methods within your lesson?	Technical Teaching	The focus of this reflective question is on how the teacher provides differentiated instructional methods. Each of these is a technical approach to the lesson. In addition, the focus is on the teacher's action, void of any reflection on evidence of student learning.

Technical Learning

This type of feedback is focused on technical aspects of the learning process such as progressive learning (showing learning over time), tracking learning (evaluating learning along the way), monitoring learning (setting benchmarks), and evidence of learning (clear demonstration of student learning). This feedback is concentrated both on teacher actions and student outcomes. Learning is the focus as the result of teacher actions, which means that the learning aspects are data driven and can be addressed quickly with clearly identifiable solutions.

Example 1

Example of Feedback	Feedback Quadrant	Rationale
How are students expected to communicate what they have learned?	Technical Learning	The focus of this reflective question is on "how students will communicate." This strategy or activity is technical. However, "what" they are expected to communicate is focused on evidence of their learning.

Example 2

Example of Feedback	Feedback Quadrant	Rationale
What strategies do you use to gather input from students during instruction? What evidence can you share that the strategies ensure all students are learning at the level of the standard?	Technical Learning	The focus of these reflective questions is on "strategies." However, the teacher is asked to reflect on and produce evidence of the impact of the strategy on student learning.

Reflective Activity 4.2:

Review the examples of how to transition Technical Teaching reflective questions into Technical Learning reflective questions. Practice on your own in Example 3.

Example 1

Example of Feedback	Feedback Quadrant	Rationale
How will the goals for learning be communicated to students?	Technical Teaching	The focus of this reflective question is on "goals" and how they will be communicated to students. Goals are technical, and the action of communicating the goals to students is a teacher action. Although the word "learning" appears in this question, there is no actual focus on the teacher's providing evidence of student learning or even reflecting on student learning.
Consideration for Improvement		
Please share evidence that all students were successful with the learning goals.	Technical Learning	The focus of this reflective question is on evidence of student learning while still requiring the teacher to reflect on the learning goals. This question also establishes an expectation that there will be follow-up based on the feedback.

Example 2

Example of Feedback	Feedback Quadrant	Rationale
How do you provide differentiated instructional methods within your lesson?	Technical Teaching	The focus of this reflective question is on how the teacher provides differentiated instructional methods. Each of these is a technical approach to the lesson. In addition, the focus is on the teacher's action, void of any reflection on evidence of student learning.
Consideration for Improvement		
Which instructional strategies proved to be the most effective at ensuring students were successful with their learning at the level of the standard?	Technical Learning	The focus of this reflective question is on evidence of student learning while still requiring the teacher to reflect on differentiated instructional strategies.

Example 3

Example of Feedback	Feedback Quadrant	Rationale
What are some strategies you use to provoke and guide discussions with students?	Technical Teaching	This reflective question is focused on strategies and teacher actions.
How would you turn that question into a Technical Learning reflective question?		

Adaptive Teaching

On the other side of the spectrum, there is feedback that falls into the adaptive-teaching quadrant. This quadrant is reserved for feedback that focuses on the adaptive nature of pedagogy (the method of practice of teaching), yet is still teacher-centered. Adaptive aspects such as belief in self, establishment of culture, learning environment, and even engaging in reflection of best practice are not easy to identify or fix. However, feedback that falls into this quadrant is absent of reflection or discussion of the eventual or immediate impact that these adaptive aspects have on student learning. The challenges that arise in each area of feedback are often ambiguous and subject to change.

Example 1

Example of Feedback	Feedback Quadrant	Rationale
How do you keep your students motivated when they have repetitive tasks?	Adaptive Teaching	The focus of this reflective question is on teacher activity. However, asking the teacher to reflect on their impact on student motivation is adaptive by nature. This question does not focus on evidence of student learning.

Example 2

Example of Feedback	Feedback Quadrant	Rationale
Think about challenges that occur when preparing the learning environment for students; how do you address obstacles?	Adaptive Teaching	The focus of this reflective question is on "challenges" and "obstacles," both of which are adaptive. Even though "students" are mentioned, the focus is on the teacher actions.

Adaptive Learning

The 4th quadrant is adaptive learning. Much like adaptive teaching, these elements of feedback are related to people, not process. They involve adaptive aspects such as emotion, relationship-building, and complex human concepts. This quadrant includes a focus on student learning to determine how students felt about learning, whether students were inspired and motivated to learn, and beliefs about learning.

Example 1:

Example of Feedback	Feedback Quadrant	Rationale
How are students encouraged to establish a culture of positive persistence, and what evidence will you be able to share that it has a positive impact on student achievement?	Adaptive Learning	The focus of this reflective question is on student culture and persistence, which are adaptive aspects. This question requires the teacher to reflect on evidence of student learning.

Example 2:

Example of Feedback	Feedback Quadrant	Rationale
How does knowledge of your students help you ensure high levels of learning, social and emotional development, and achievement for all your students? What evidence supports your statement?	Adaptive Learning	The focus of this reflective question is on an adaptive aspect of knowing and understanding the students. This question is followed up by a reflection on evidence of the impact of this knowledge on learning.

Reflective Activity 4.3:

Review the examples of how to transition Adaptive Teaching reflective questions into Adaptive Learning reflective questions. Practice on your own in Example 3.

Example 1:

Example of Feedback	Feedback Quadrant	Rationale
How do you keep your students motivated when they have repetitive tasks?	Adaptive Teaching	The focus of this reflective question is on teacher activity. However, asking the teacher to reflect on their impact on student motivation is adaptive by nature. This question does not focus on evidence of student learning.
Consideration for Improvement		
How are you motivating students to stay engaged, and what impact is such motivation having on their learning? What evidence supports this?	Adaptive Learning	The focus of this reflective question is on evidence of student learning while still requiring the teacher to reflect on their ability to motivate students.

Example 2:

Example of Feedback	Feedback Quadrant	Rationale
Think about challenges that occur when preparing the learning environment for students; how do you address obstacles?	Adaptive Teaching	The focus of this reflective question is on "challenges" and "obstacles," both of which are adaptive. Even though "students" are mentioned, the focus is on the teacher actions.
Consideration for Improvement		
How did the learning environment engage, challenge, and encourage student learning? What evidence of student learning supports this?	Adaptive Learning	The focus of the questions is on adaptive aspects of the learning environment that affect student learning. By asking for evidence of impact, it keeps the reflection grounded on student achievement.

Example 3:

Example of Feedback	Feedback Quadrant	Rationale
In what ways are students expected to take initiative for their own learning? What role do you play in this?	Adaptive Teaching	The focus of the questions is on the teacher's role of communicating expectations for students taking "initiative" for their own learning. The questions do not focus on evidence of student learning.
How would you turn that question into an Adaptive Learning reflective question?		

After I reviewed hundreds of feedback evaluations based on these walk-throughs and categorized the feedback into one of these four "types," I made a startling discovery.

Nearly all the feedback was focused on teaching, both technical and adaptive...but mostly technical. I gathered local data from four urban school districts with student populations ranging from 8,564 to 63,451 students. Their economically disadvantaged populations ranged from 43.7% to 89.2% of their total populations. The average professional experience of the schools' principals ranged from 3.4 years to 6.6 years. It turned out that over 50% of all feedback for teachers was about technical teaching, while only 2% was about adaptive learning. Moreover, 12% of the time, feedback was not provided to the teacher at all. By overemphasizing technical teaching feedback, too few are talking about the adaptive aspects of learning. If schools are institutions of learning and our goal as leaders is to ensure learning…that wasn't happening. How can we ensure learning when the majority of feedback is focused on teaching? We can't. Because without proper and timely feedback about learning, teachers can't ensure learning. Yet administrators have no problem with providing abundant feedback on teaching.

Why? Well, it is easier to tell teachers to plan faster, collaborate harder, and run their lessons more efficiently. However, it is possible to have the greatest lesson plan, finite alignment, and unparalleled pacing, and for students to still not learn.

Teachers need to be empowered to meet with their administrators and request feedback on learning. Leaders need to realize that while technical is easy, it is not always the most beneficial challenge to tackle when you want to ensure learning throughout your institution. Remember, what you spend time on grows. So, if administrators are spending all their time providing feedback on technical issues…well, technical issues are going to grow.

Feedback should not tell teachers what to do. Feedback should guide teachers to come up with solutions and help them in the thinking process. After all, adaptive challenges are the hardest to pinpoint but the easiest to deny. Yet, the people involved in the challenge are tasked with finding a solution.

A building full of processors will always outperform people who have to have the answers. Just like a classroom full of learners will always outperform a classroom of students.

Reflective Activity 4.4: "Where Is Your Focus?"

Reflect on which of the following ideas you hold true.

Focused on Teaching	Focused on Learning
☐ Respect is earned.	☐ Respect is given, regardless of how it is received.
☐ Student work must be submitted on time in order to obtain full credit.	☐ Student demonstration of mastery should be awarded full credit regardless of how long it takes.
☐ It is my responsibility to provide the information. It is their responsibility to learn it.	☐ It is my responsibility to ensure learning.
☐ They need to understand me.	☐ I need to understand them.
☐ Start with the "What."	☐ Start with the "Why."
☐ I rarely, if ever, engage in discussion pertaining to evidence of student learning.	☐ I always engage in discussion pertaining to evidence of student learning.
☐ Topics, lessons, and discussions should be teacher driven.	☐ Topics, lessons, and discussions should be student driven.
☐ Assessments should be used to monitor learning.	☐ Assessments should be used to promote and diagnose learning.
☐ I answer questions and offer advice.	☐ I probe reflective thinking in others.
☐ I establish a culture of competitiveness.	☐ I establish a culture of collaboration and support.
☐ I emphasize correct answers.	☐ I emphasize generating better questions and learning from mistakes.

Key Points

- Assessments and evaluation are not the same. Assessment involves giving timely, detailed feedback based around clearly defined learning outcomes. Evaluation is giving a grade to a piece of work, usually based on normative criteria, but too often compared to the work of other students.

- There are two types of mindsets: fixed and growth. The growth mindset is where we should strive to be. It embraces flexibility and change.

- There are two types of challenges: technical and adaptive. Technical challenges have quick, obvious solutions and can be solved by an expert or authority. Adaptive challenges have ambiguous, ever-changing, complex solutions and must be solved by the people who have the challenge.

- In education, most administrators give feedback on technical teaching and adaptive teaching, while failing to provide constructive, quality feedback on learning. For schools to ensure learning, teachers need to be given feedback and guided to ensure learning. Less focus needs to be put on the teacher, and more focus needs to illuminate learning.

- Feedback should always conclude by providing teachers an opportunity to reflect on evidence of student learning.

CHAPTER 5 - SUSTAINABLE ACHIEVEMENT WITH SIX SIMPLE STEPS

"We have to learn to think in a new way."

– Albert Einstein

As an assistant principal, I was highly effective in working with the social studies department to improve student achievement. After all, I was previously a great social studies teacher. I understood the state standards, pulled from my experience with challenging classes, and was so comfortable with the curriculum that I could easily guide my social studies department through any instructional mishaps they might have faced. For so long I had relied on my comfort level that I neglected to adhere to the research on best practice for data-driven instruction, instructional planning, and managing school leadership teams. What I did as an assistant principal worked for my team and me, so why would I bother with reading, understanding, and implementing researched-based best practice? I thought I knew all that I needed to know!

But once I became a principal, I was responsible for the growth and development of an entire school. I knew good instruction, but my inability to understand the nuances of research-based practices to support quality data-driven instruction in all areas immediately exposed my deficiencies. As a result, it took much longer to define and develop the roadmap for teaching to meet the students' needs. It also took longer to train instructional leaders to expand my impact across the school and create a strong culture where learning could thrive.

Research alone does not change practice. That statement is true in every field, be it engineering, education, or law. Studies are not enough to change the day-to-day practice and habits of professionals. Just putting information into someone's hands does not help them understand how to use that information in order to improve their work. But empowering yourself and your team to best understand trustworthy, well-designed, and well-executed research founded on proven results can better prepare you and your team for sustained success.

There is a fascinating book by Marshall Goldsmith called *What Got You Here Won't Get You There: How Successful People Become Even More Successful*. Goldsmith says the research and practices that an individual uses to obtain a higher-level leadership role are not necessarily the tools one needs once that role is achieved.

In the educational leadership arena, talented assistant principals are often promoted to the role of principal when the opportunity comes. Most often, assistant principals are promoted because they were great at what they did. They supported district and campus initiatives with a positive attitude, managed student discipline, supported improvement in their academic department, managed the operations of the school, and effectively interacted with various stakeholders. A promotion based on previous performance—based on how good someone *was*—does not always translate into how good they *will be* in a new leadership role. Simply put, what got you here won't get you there.

The newly minted principal faces an entirely new position. There are more people to manage, the scope of the work is new, the responsibilities are different, the time commitment is bigger, the priorities are unique, and the consequences of decisions made have a greater impact.

The new principal must make decisions that positively affect students, faculty, and stakeholders while factoring in the political aspects of their decision. Welcome to the leadership thinking game. If that new principal falls back solely on his or her past experiences as an assistant principal, the guidance and answers to leadership situations may not always be relevant.

What does one do when faced with a problem one does not have the experience to solve?

The answer is research. The educational leadership arena is filled with best practices, tenants of leadership, case studies, and more. Every new leader knows he or she can research tools for success. But every new leader does not always put those tools into practice.

It is called *the research-practice gap*. It is a gap where leaders know what the research says, but they fail to implement the best practices from that research. Principals say the gap occurs due to a "prevailing sense of urgency" and "a lack of time," compounded by "scheduling demands." Instead of relying on the evidence-based research to conquer everyday leadership situations, principals feel forced to react to the situations rather than respond.

The research-practice gap is relatively universal. Airline pilots early in their careers spend a lot of time thinking about flying and learning how to fly. Veteran pilots spend less time in the "thinking" zone and more time "doing." In his paper, "How Expert Pilots Think: Cognitive Processes in Expert Decision Making," Richard J. Adams states, "The mechanism behind this transition is not clearly understood and typically it has been assumed that learning to make good decisions could only be achieved through experience." Veteran principals, like seasoned pilots, operate in the "doing" zone, but those who are new to the job struggle.

When first-time principals credit scheduling demands, lack of time, and urgency as the root cause of the research-practice gap, they are not making up excuses. These are very real problems.

There is a huge demand placed upon principals and the profession itself. When the time comes, principals are expected to have the answer, to know what to do, to make the decision and to move forward. Principals hire new teachers and staff, complete employee evaluations, develop professional-development programs, and build the culture within a school. Those demands and that urgency create the perception of "I don't have time to engage in a process of thought because I have to give an answer and a solution."

It is worth mentioning that the aforementioned tendency applies to nonemergency decisions. Clearly, when safety is a factor or an emergency situation arises, principals are absolutely expected to react and follow their protocols and gut intuitions to mitigate the situation. But most issues that we're talking about here aren't emergencies. They are decisions that invite leaders to think, process, and consider multiple perspectives.

Those decisions could center around planning professional development, professional learning community meetings, effective teacher evaluations, interventions for student achievement, or even something as simple as helping teachers understand the lesson-plan process.

Leadership Is the Art of Processing

Principals are responsible for so much, and an inability to respond in a timely manner can have a tremendous negative impact on the organization. The harsh consequences of poor decision-making on the part of the principal permeate through the entire organization—all the principal's inefficiencies flow downstream to assistant principals, teachers, and students.

The research-practice gap bleeds into other areas. It can make a principal reliant on emulating the same practices they always have, choosing comfort over more efficient ideas.

A significant challenge to educational leaders today is that more often than not, they think the same way they always did. They fail to lean into researched best practices. They take the path they've traveled before. That response is human nature, because we crave comfort, and leaders are rarely exposed to the right way to engage in a thought process.

So, we end up with leaders who rely on "what worked before" in a previous role. We have leaders encumbered by a prevailing sense of urgency, having to put out fires left and right in the most reactive manner. We have leaders responding to their environment. We have leaders who have not been exposed to an evidence-based way of "thought processing" for decision-making. As a result, such leaders lack the ability to empower others through the art of strategic processing.

So, what can leaders—any principal, novice, and veteran—do to reduce the research-practice gap and implement conscious and analytical decision-making? Make them sky-bound!

The Leadership Cycle

Of course, I don't mean that literally, but the solution is upward.

Research conducted on Aeronautical Decision Making (ADM) proved that pilot behavior is not only learned, but can be developed over time through structured training and strategic thought processes. The ADM thought process was implemented and studied. As it turns out, a 48.2% reduction of Human Performance Error accidents in the U.S. occurred, compared to before ADM was implemented. A 72.3% reduction in accidents from weather-related decisions also occurred.

The ADM thought process worked. It was a strategic process with concrete steps, each step informing the next. Today, it is widely practiced and contributes to aeronautical safety.

Effective principals may not be piloting aircrafts, but they are certainly piloting their schools. The educational training principles from the ADM that we as educators can adopt are found in the leadership cycle. It is similar to the process pilots now rely on, and is a six-step proven process of thinking and implementation.

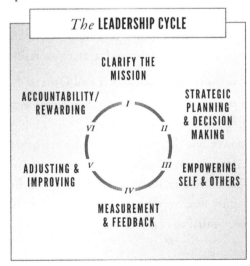

The **LEADERSHIP CYCLE**

CLARIFY THE MISSION

ACCOUNTABILITY/ REWARDING

STRATEGIC PLANNING & DECISION MAKING

ADJUSTING & IMPROVING

EMPOWERING SELF & OTHERS

MEASUREMENT & FEEDBACK

Like any cycle, the steps must be completed in order, so that results and alignment among teachers and faculty are achieved. Go out of order, and you will face negative consequences. The Leadership Cycle is incredibly simple. Yes, it takes time to process through, but it is worth the investment. By engaging in each step, leaders will make strategic and conscious decisions every single time. Throughout this book, you will find chapters dedicated to each step of the Leadership Cycle. But to get started, here is a brief introduction to what we'll be covering:

1. **Step One: Clarify the Mission: Don't just "share." Ensure understanding.**

   The very first step in the Leadership Cycle is to clarify the mission. When we say clarify, we do not mean tell, share, or give. We do not mean email or drop off a memo. There is a big difference between clarifying and sharing. To clarify means to ensure understanding. It means you have taken time to garner that understanding and ensure that the person to whom you have delivered the message has comprehended what you are trying to communicate.

2. **Step Two: Strategic Planning and Decision-Making**

   People may ask, "What is the difference between planning and strategic planning?" Strategic planning involves conscious and analytical decision-making. It is detailed, calculated, and clearly defined, like that 30,000-foot view of implementation. Both are important, but one will lead to more effective and sustainable results than the other.

3. **Step Three: Empowerment of Self and Others**

   The third step in the Leadership Cycle is Empowerment of Self and Others. John C. Maxwell says, "Leaders become great not because of their power but their ability to empower others." If you're not growing, if you're not learning, if you're not a consumer of information in a proactive way, then you're going to be behind the eight ball and constantly react to your environment. Your ability to empower yourself is essential to empower others.

4. **Step Four: Measurement and Feedback**

It goes without saying, but what you do not monitor, you do not improve. People grow through effective feedback.

Sadly, that step is where most leaders really drop the ball. They might clarify the mission. They will be strategic with planning. Those leaders empower themselves and others. But they fall short putting systems in place to measure, monitor, and even provide quality feedback.

When a situation arises that may not have yielded the intended outcome, I will often accompany leaders through this leadership process and ask them to walk me through each step. When we get to step four, I will ask, "How did you monitor and measure the feedback given?" Often, measurement and quality feedback are missing.

5. **Step Five: Adjusting and Improving**

Growth will result when you adjust and improve. Once you monitor and provide feedback, what action steps are you taking based on that monitoring and feedback? You do not want to remain stagnant, and you surely do not want to go through all of the steps of the Leadership Cycle just to foster no change or progress. That ending would be a waste of investment in your time and others'.

When you adjust and improve based on your system for providing and monitoring feedback, you will start to notice a huge progressive push forward. That forward movement goes for everything you, as a leader, do—school budgets, lesson plans, professional development, you name it. Everything can be adjusted and improved accordingly with the right feedback in place. Much like leadership itself, adjustment and improving is a way of thinking.

But it can be learned, and it can be celebrated.

6. **Step Six: Accountability and Rewarding**

The final step of the Leadership Cycle is Accountability and Rewarding, which is where the level of support you have provided justifies the level of accountability or celebration of success that people should expect. You want to foster a culture of accountability within your school. That position means that everyone knows what is expected of them (because you clarified the mission), they take ownership of their responsibilities, they received quality feedback for development and growth, and they had the opportunity to make the necessary adjustments to improve and meet the expectations.

You get what you tolerate. What you celebrate will duplicate.

What Happens If You Skip a Step in the Leadership Cycle?

If one of these steps is missing, the probability of your being successful diminishes. Let's explore why with the following example.

The first step, clarifying the mission, must precede the rest of the Leadership Cycle. Without understanding what must be done, how can you and your team possibly know how to proceed? The second step, strategic planning and decision-making, can only be successful if first the mission is clarified. You cannot lay out a blueprint if it is not clear what you are building! The third step, empowering yourself and others, can only be achieved once the mission is understood and the strategy is outlined. Otherwise, it would be impossible to know what you'd need to do in order to empower all of the relevant players. The 4th step, providing measurement feedback, necessarily comes after everyone is aligned with the mission and is empowered in their role. Now that everyone is on the same page and begins to work toward the goal, feedback should be given so that they can make the appropriate adjustments. The cycle brings us to the 5th step, adjusting and improving, which can only come once people integrate feedback into their actions. Adjusting needs to be done with a purpose, rather than "on a whim." The final step, accountability and rewarding, makes no sense unless it comes after the previous steps. A leader cannot hold his or her subordinates accountable if the mission is not clear, if feedback is not given, if they do not feel empowered. However, if everyone is working toward the mission and they know what must be done, accountability is appreciated by all parties.

Let's say you ensured clarity with the mission, strategically planned, and empowered yourself and others. Then you provided professional development, reminders of the purpose to ensure student learning, and established a highly effective professional learning community. Despite those efforts, a teacher continues to struggle with classroom management. It may seem justified to document that teacher's inability to improve. After all you cannot have a poorly engaged group of students, right?

The failure is not aligned with the mission. Your teacher is not empowering the students. Clearly something has to be done.

Sure, you're holding someone accountable, but how will such haphazard decision-making eventually affect your culture? Did you deploy the proper systems to engage in timely quality feedback? If the behavior has continued for months on end, why are you just now addressing it? Proper monitoring, targeted support, and quality feedback on the part of leadership is crucial. If you skip past steps four and five, heading down the fast lane to step six, you will not get the result you intended.

Have you had prior conversations with that teacher to find ways to foster improvement and development? Or did you assume she knew the expectations set forth on the first day of school and just clearly failed to meet them?

As you can see, the Cycle of Leadership, when not followed in order, looks like a circle of Swiss cheese, full of holes and confusion. Had you proceeded through each step, in order, you would have discovered an opportunity to provide timely and relevant feedback to that teacher and set a system to monitor that feedback, adjusting accordingly. Sometimes corrective actions are necessary, but that method of management is rarely the "easy" button it seems to be. It is reactive, sometimes downright impulsive. Not only that, but the quick-hit method of reprimand will not create a sustainable environment for success.

Creating a Sustainable Environment for Success

The beauty of the Leadership Cycle is that it is just that, a cycle. As you practice and deploy these steps, you'll begin to see how they all are interconnected. In time, the Leadership Cycle will become second nature, with each step guiding you to the next. While it may challenge your patience and thinking at first, it is a surefire way to foster growth and change in your school.

It is proven. It is based on research. It is effective. However, it is not the Leadership Cycle itself that is proven, but the brilliant results that are born from a comprehensive thought process like the Leadership Cycle.

The key is to create a sustainable environment for success. You don't want to do one-off solutions, which is like putting a Band-Aid on a wound that requires stitches. You want to go all in and really complete the transformational thinking process to solidify lasting and sustainable change within your organization. You want to make decisions that stick in the best possible way, and the Leadership Cycle is a proven way to make it happen.

After all, how much is a decision worth? Decisions can cost you everything or nothing, but indecision can be even costlier. When we choose to not make the right decision, not reflect, not employ best practices, it will cost us more than we are willing to pay.

Over the next few chapters, we're going to dive a little deeper into each step of the Leadership Cycle. By the completion of this book, my hope is that you will firmly believe that everything you need to foster change within your school is written in these pages—and ultimately within you too.

Reflective Activity 5.1: "Leadership Cycle Analysis"

Respond to each statement as honestly and accurately as possible as they relate to your own school, with 1 indicating rarely (or never) practiced and 5 indicating consistent practice:

Leadership Cycle Statement	1	2	3	4	5
Ensuring Clarity					
Our leadership team makes a clear distinction between providing information and ensuring clarity of provided information.					
We provide frequent opportunities for people to demonstrate their understanding of provided information.					
Impacted personnel is consistently clear about the what, why, when, and how.					

Strategic Planning and Decision-Making					
We are strategic when planning and are prepared for multiple scenarios.					
We consistently involve the people impacted by the decisions in the planning process.					
We consistently make informed decisions that lead to clearly defined action steps.					
Planning meetings are consistently purposeful, effective, and efficient.					
Empowering Self and Others					
We consistently provide people with an opportunity to engage with information in relation to the desired impact of the mission.					
We are consistently reading, researching, and implementing best practice.					
Our leadership team consistently models a growth mindset.					
We value improvement in others and prioritize their success.					
Measurement and Feedback					
We regularly monitor the quality of feedback being provided.					
Quality feedback is frequently provided to inform for improvement.					
We consistently measure what is expected and make proper adjustments in a timely manner.					
Everyone is clear about monitoring and measurement metrics including timelines for improvement.					
We regularly review feedback provided to measure impact.					
Adjustment and Improvement					
We regularly make timely adjustments when we see lack of improvement.					

We regularly identify root causes that impede improvement.				
Our organization consistently buys in when we need to make adjustments.				
Accountability and Rewarding				
People at all levels have a clear sense of direction, purpose, and priorities rather than dealing with fragmented, competing, or overwhelming priorities.				
Everyone in the organization takes ownership of mistakes.				
Poor performers are addressed, coached, supported, or removed instead of ignored, transferred, or promoted.				
People are regularly acknowledged and recognized for their value and contribution as opposed to relying on formal/structured recognitions or awards.				

89 or Higher	High Results indicating lots of quality leadership decisions. Scores in this range indicate real, influential leadership and organizational strengths as well as areas that may need some focused improvement. High probability of ensuring success!
44 – 88	Average Results - indicating ineffectiveness in decision-making. Lower probability of ensuring success.
43 or Lower	Low Results - indicating a clear issue with ensuring success.

Key Points

- There is a research-performance gap where leaders fail to deploy best practices from research to their daily decision-making.

- The pressure and responsibility placed upon principals is huge and contributes to the perception that there is a "sense of urgency" with everything, dissuading principals from engaging in analytical thought processes.

- The Leadership Cycle is a proven thought process made of six steps:

1. Clarify the Mission

2. Strategic Planning and Decision-Making

3. Empowerment of Self and Others

4. Measurement and Feedback

5. Adjusting and Improving

6. Accountability and Rewarding

CHAPTER 6 - CLARITY

"The single biggest problem in
communication is the illusion that it has taken place."

— William H. Whyte

Let us explore the very first step of the Leadership Cycle and how effective educational leaders put it in place. I touched on that aspect briefly in the overview of the Leadership Cycle. Before we discuss the mission, we must first develop a deep understanding on what it means **to clarify.**

When you clarify the mission, you make sure everyone shares a common sense of direction born from a unified purpose. The leader establishes the vision, which then guides the mission. As a leader, you ensure clarity, and you ensure understanding of the expectations of your teams throughout your school. Everyone is on the same page. Everyone understands what is expected. Everyone is clear about the commitment to support as well as the levels of accountability when expectations are not met. Everyone is inspired by the forward-thinking goals that you, as the leader, have brought to light.

As leaders, we have to recognize that the burden of clarity always rests on the communicator. Effective leaders are master communicators and must be committed to ensuring a mutual understanding. Several different tactics can be used to accomplish clarity.

Here is the high-level list of steps that one should take to ensure clarity:

1. Establish a vision.

2. Be specific.

3. Share your vision.

4. Hold your team accountable.

5. Be consistent.

The very first step to ensure clarity and mutual understanding is to be specific, which means refraining from using ambiguous and extraneous vocabulary. Take the word "check," for example. How many different meanings exist for this word? It can mean to look after a person, place, or thing. It can be a form of payment. It can even be the bill after dining at a restaurant. It can mean the symbol on a piece of paper in a tiny box. One tiny word has many different meanings, and each meaning is based on the experience of the person with whom you are communicating. Those individual experiences have shaped the listener's perception and understanding of words that may be perceived as ambiguous. There are so many words that potentially have multiple meanings.

Take a moment to consider multiple meanings for the following: *turn, keep, round, see, sound, stick, square.* Recognizing the use of, and the need to define, ambiguous terms is key to effective communication. In the educational realm, there is one word that has a myriad of meanings, and teachers tend to use it a lot. That word is "respect."

Teachers have a habit of saying, "The child did not respect me," but what is respect? If we lined up a room full of teachers and asked that question, I assure you we would get a variety of answers. Each individual would pull from their unique experiences and exposures and provide a definition in concert with those encounters. Thus, the teachers' experiences would shape their perspective of what it means to be respectful.

How to Ensure Clarity

The foundation of clarity is to establish mutual understanding. One way is to simply ask a question at the conclusion of your clarifying statement:

"Would you mind sharing with me what you're taking away from our conversation?"

The person with whom you are communicating will then share with you what was important to them—the information that sticks in their memory. The revelation will provide you with all you need to know about what information was important to *them*. Now, it is your turn to listen closely. Are they sharing things you didn't intend to be a priority? If so, you will need to ensure clarity once more. This layer of verification goes far beyond asking, "Do you understand?" A question prompting a yes or no answer does not ensure clarity, but it might ensure compliance.

Asking your listener to share their takeaways from your conversation is very simple but produces powerful results. This manner of questioning is not defensive. It is nonintrusive. There is an undercurrent message that says, *I care enough about you to ensure clarity.* It is empowering for both parties. Like most skills in life, the more you practice that method of communicating, the easier it will get, and the more expected it will become.

As leaders, we all have different tools for communicating. In today's fast-paced, technologically savvy world, we rely heavily on email and text messages. While these methods of communication are convenient in a pinch, the problem is you can never really detect a person's tone through the text presented. You miss out on your listener's body language. A huge percentage of our communication is nonverbal. Therefore, as listeners, we miss a lot of good information when we choose to communicate through email and text messages.

The following are several reflective questions you can use in your electronic communications to ensure clarity:

- How many times and in how many ways will I communicate this message?

- Is the context of this communication appropriate, relevant, and in alignment with my intended message?

- What feedback will I seek for acknowledgement, clarification, and understanding?

- What possible misconceptions could this message generate and how can I avoid those misconceptions?

- Am I in an emotionally intelligent state to share this message at the moment? Is my tone and mood appropriate at this time to share this message electronically?

Remember, the focus of communication is not what is being said, texted, or emailed. It is what is being understood. Take the time to reflect. Ending with a request to summarize understanding is how you ensure clarity.

Vision before Mission

In order to clarify the mission, you first need a vision. A vision is a manifestation of a future direction. It is never what is, but rather what could be. A vision points you in a direction, but doesn't tell you exactly what to do to get there. Despite that vagueness, the vision cannot be nebulous. The vision cannot be a 300-page dissertation.

A vision is a way to picture the future using one's imagination and wisdom. A vision is something that doesn't exist quite yet. Fundamentally, leadership is all about seeing and creating a brighter future. Leaders invent, innovate, create, build, improve, and develop every aspect of our lives and the world around us. Educational leaders are tasked with the never-ending responsibility to innovate and transform the educational experience. Sometimes, that commitment requires some big ideas and out-of-the-box thinking, dreaming, and imagination to create the future and change the world.

Who better to lay the groundwork for the vision than the leader?

Most leadership-development books will tell you something different. They will say that it is up to the team to establish the vision with the leader and then carry that vision out through the collaboratively established mission statement. Collaborative vision development will foster a sense of ownership and buy-in, therefore everyone should have a say.

I respectfully disagree.

How to Use the Vision to Inspire

Positive leaders tap into the power of a vision. They use this power to determine a way forward. In order to inspire, motivate, and rally others to follow your lead, you must be able to articulate your vision in a clear and compelling manner. You must ensure clarity and inspire others.

All effective leaders know that inspiration is a valuable leadership tool, but inspiration itself must be organized and targeted. A leader has the capacity to help people to bypass the present, to catch a vision of the future, and obtain the ticket and ride to get there.

When Martin Luther King Jr., at a very young age, assumed the responsibility to lead what we now call the Civil Rights Movement, he was incredibly inspired by Mahatma Gandhi's vision for nonviolent social change. Martin Luther King Jr. would go on to inspire a burdened, abused, disenfranchised, beaten generation to achieve justice and equality through nonviolence and hope. The entire movement was completely reliant on King's ability to motivate, inspire, encourage, and elicit that hope when there was no hope to be found.

Dr. King had a vision of what could be. He did not meet with the delegates of the National Association for the Advancement of Colored People (NAACP) and ask them to *collaborate* on his vision, his dream, his passion for his children and the plight of African Americans under constant oppression. Dr. King had a dream, and he shared it. He shared it again in front of 260,000 people at the March on Washington, in what is widely considered the greatest speech of the 20th Century.

That action is the difference between sharing a vision and seeking collaboration on a vision. Dr. King articulated that dream even knowing that he might never witness its conception. He said so himself, in another inspiring speech that he made the day before he was assassinated: "I may not get there with you." Still, he used his words and his hope to ignite a passionate fire throughout a divided nation. He lived each day with passion, conviction, and commitment, and he inspired people to catch his vision. Today, we're still trying to catch that vision.

Can you imagine an African American man sitting at the dinner table with his wife and two young children? His family has witnessed nothing but division, segregation, and being "less than." After being inspired and motivated by Dr. King's vision, the man turns to his wife and says, "I am aware of the present laws of segregation, but I'm going to sit in a restaurant tomorrow. I am uncertain of what this will mean for me personally, and I do not know if I will be back. I don't know if I will be harassed, beaten, or arrested. I do know that there will be a heavy price to pay for what I plan to do. But I'm going there not because I am allowed. I'm going so they will be allowed." He glances at his children. "I want to endure this, so they don't have to."

It takes extraordinary vision to encourage people to walk right into the mouths of biting dogs, which is exactly what Dr. King did. With the only weapon being a heart of hope, Dr. King spread a message of what life could be.

Winston Churchill, Nelson Mandela, Barack Obama and Rosa Parks are just a few other extraordinary individuals who have shared their visions and inspired millions. Messages of hope are contagious. The first commitment of leadership should be to inspire people toward the vision. A leader is always considering what could be, while everyone else considers w*hat is.* Leaders are always going to be pulling people with them to understand, to catch, to buy into, and to see the vision they have.

Educational leaders face the same expectations. Obstacles may not be life or death, but they surely exist. From policies to procedures to funding to different personalities to regional and state accreditations…the list goes on and on. But all it takes is one effective leader with a heartfelt, bold, and transformational passion to radiate possibility and change with every conversation. That ability is what our extraordinary leaders of history have in common with our effective leaders today. It starts with the leader.

Too often, leaders come into schools and try to establish a vision with the people. They say, "Okay, what is important to the collective 'us,' and how are we going to get there?" Everyone chimes in. The school seems to be on the same page as to what the vision is and how missions will carry that vision out.

But what happens when there is a change of leadership, or a change of staff? What happens when four teachers retire, and three new teachers are hired straight out of college? Do you gather everyone together and reestablish a vision with the new parties present? Do you continue with the previously defined vision and hope the new additions buy in to something constructed before their arrival? That choice can get messy and take a lot of time. Also, it brings the vision into the "present moment" instead of the future.

Leaders do not establish a vision with the people. Leaders are catalysts for establishing missions with people. Vision is where you are going. When people leave, that vision doesn't change, the goal doesn't change and the audacity of hope doesn't change. Keeping that continuity isn't to say that leaders know more. That resolution is not about ego. It is about being passionate, purposeful, and taking something from where it is to where it can be.

As you address your teachers and staff, you should share your vision. Remember the cornerstones of ensuring clarity. Then ask the question, "What does this vision mean to you?" First, as I mentioned before, you will be able to identify what is important to that individual based on their response. Second, for a vision to come to life, it must have meaning to people individually. You must take the time to ask that question and really listen to the answer.

With that understanding established, ask your teachers and staff about their personal visions and how they can contribute to the bigger vision of the organization. You may just find a few mini-missions as you listen intently and really hear what your teams have to share. But the conversation doesn't stop there. You, the leader, are responsible for helping your people reach their personal visions. You can do it by asking what they need from you to be their absolute best. They may not have the answers right away, but be sure to follow up.

To ensure that a vision catches on, a little accountability goes a long way. Ask your teams how they would like you to hold them accountable to their personal visions. If you have a teacher who wants to start a new science club by the following semester and have a roster of at least 15 students, be the leader who paves the way for guideposts, check-ins, and celebrations of progress.

Visions come to life through actions. It takes open, honest conversations full of clarity on personal and organization visions *throughout the year.* This process isn't a one-and-done, check-the-box activity. Think about how you start a fire. It takes kindling, air, and a spark. To grow the fire, you must feed it. It requires air and more twigs and eventually logs. A vision is just like a fire. It takes time, honest conversations, and accountability to grow and take hold.

When people know their role and their contributions to a larger vision, establish a more meaningful purpose at work, and feel like their leader genuinely cares about them, engagement soars.

Let's Talk about Missions

If the vision focuses on tomorrow and what the organization wants to become, then the mission focuses on today and what an organization does to achieve it. Both the vision and mission are vital to achieving success. The leader must turn the vision into a set of focused outcomes and develop time-based goals, structure, and an action plan. This is the mission.

When we are thinking of missions, we're thinking of all the approaches needed to accomplish a task. Anything you are asking someone to do can be clarified as a mission. Anything you're trying to accomplish could be classified as a mission. Anytime you're taking an action step toward teaching, learning, or safety, those steps themselves could be considered missions. In fact, the mission is often made up of mini-missions that support the vision.

Ancient Roman philosopher Seneca said, "If a man knows not which harbor he seeks, any wind is the right wind. You must know for which harbor you are headed if you are to catch the right wind to get you there." If you don't have a common, agreed-upon destination, you are going to yield unfocused results. The common understanding of the destination allows everyone to align their improvement efforts. Time is the only cost in deciding where you want to go. Missions give strong motivations and provide us with a clear picture of what we value. Missions are the winds to our harbor vision.

Clarifying the Mission

Once the leader has established a vision, it is time for the team to clarify the mission and subsequent mini-missions. With each mission, both big and small, the leader must ask, "Why does this need to be done? Who is responsible? What needs to be done? When will this take place? When will we know that we have accomplished the mission? How is our progress being measured?" The leader is creating the framework to ensure the desired impact of the mission is accomplished.

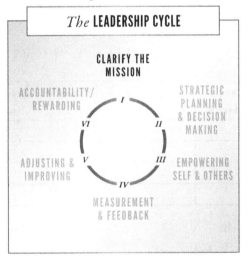

The mission can be anything from developing a tardy policy for a school to developing safety protocols to developing quality staff meetings.

Think about it: If the school's vision is to be an excellent organization that ensures quality learning, how is the tardy policy aligned with that vision? A comprehensive tardy policy maximizes instruction time, minimizes distraction, and allows staff to utilize their time effectively to contribute to the vision. Even the smallest mini-missions matter. Mini-missions inspire people to adopt positive behaviors and achieve a greater vision.

From ensuring clarity to establishing a mission, it all comes back to the people. Effective leaders must lean into their people's experiences. Everyone has something to offer. It is up to you, the leader, to help them see that too. Sometimes, helping people see their potential starts by acknowledging their potential. When we give people a vision, space to develop the mission(s), and ensure clarity along the way, the unlimited potential of our teams will be unlocked. In other words, when people see what can be accomplished and know where they are going, they will provide ideas and talents to help the organization get there.

Reflective Activity 6.1: "Determining Mission Clarity"

List a few priority missions. List supporting evidence that proves the ranking of your level of clarity that you chose, to ensure a higher level of clarity.

LEVELS OF CLARITY

1. Very Poor 2. Poor 3. Average 4. Good 5. Excellent

Mission	Level of Clarity	Supporting Evidence	Actions Steps to Ensure Clarity

Fostering Buy-In

To unlock unlimited potential for the mission(s), you will need collective buy-in. In his book *Buy-In*, Harvard business school professor John Kotter states that the process we use to secure buy-in is inherently flawed. We rarely approach it as a buy-in at all.

In fact, we typically approach new ideas with a sell-in mentality. First, we "sell" the idea or opportunity to ourselves. Then we ponder the ways people will resist the idea and develop airtight defenses to debunk their concerns.

Effective leaders need others to be open to our influence. When people feel sold to, they will resist new ideas. Simply put, people will not support what they do not understand. There are a few things we can do to garner buy-in when it comes to the mission:

1. *Engage in transparent and honest dialogue.* In his book *Good to Great,* Jim Collins says, "Successful leaders infuse the entire decision-making process with the brutal facts of reality" (Pinelli, Nicole). By going beyond the data, the reasons, and tapping into others' emotions, effective leaders can make great strides toward a transparent and honest dialogue. Use vivid and compelling examples to illustrate your point. Talk to your people about what can happen if you do and do not employ specific ideas. Take note of the visionary leaders we know and love. Did they speak from the heart? Did they paint an accurate picture of what was to come? Both transparency and honesty can go a long way as you garner buy-in from your teams.

2. *Chunking.* The introduction to any type of change initiative can seem overwhelming at first. After all, many people are resistant to change. To reduce the effect on your team of being overwhelmed, you can break down your change initiatives into distinct phases and steps. Be sure to include interim goals to keep you on track. That simplicity makes the impossible very possible. As the saying goes, "How do you eat an elephant? One bite at a time."

3. *Simply listening.* Rick Maurer's book *Why Don't You Do What I Want?* has a powerful quote that says, "Relationships are as important as ideas." If you are going to ensure clarity, then you want to make sure you are an effective listener as well. Truly listening to others is a way to build relationships. By listening, you can also identify if your team is resistant to change.

   Maurer classifies resistance to change in three broad categories: (1) I don't get it, (2) I don't like it, and (3) I don't like you. The first category invites you to ensure understanding, whereas the second two categories are emotional reactions to the change or the messenger of change, which is why listening is so important. The more you know, the better you can take steps to listen fully and help your teammates discover the root of their change resistance.

4. *Obtaining feedback and input.* By and large, one of the biggest challenges is when administration drives change using the top-down approach. All new ideas, missions, and opportunities come from above and trickle down the "pyramid." That practice is a death sentence to your organization. It says that whoever is at the top "knows it all." That isn't leadership. You have to get feedback to understand the dynamics of your team and obtain input on how to collectively fulfill each mini-mission to make the vision come to life. Research tells us that people who ask for advice are seen as more credible, so ask.

5. *Communicating progress.* When we fail to communicate progress, enthusiasm will wane and buy-in dissipates. If we listen, share, communicate, make goals, obtain input, and adjust, but we fail to provide communication on our progress, we lose credibility, transparency, and collaborative investment. People feel like part of the solution if you keep updating them on the progress you are making together.

So, we listen. We share the vision. We communicate the missions born out of the vision. We make the goals. We put in the processes and changes needed to meet those goals. We take all of those actions, but for some reason we fail to provide communication on the progress. It will all fall apart. You either need to set benchmarks for your goals or mark quarterly times to report back and host a conversation about the status of the organization's goals. Transparency is essential.

Consistency Matters

We talked about how to ensure clarity, the difference between the vision and mission, and how to garner buy-in as a leader. In Galatians 6:7, it says, "A man reaps what he sows." The scripture couldn't apply more to successful leaders. If there is no action in cultivating efforts, just like a farmer neglecting his crops, there is no harvest. If a leader is not consistent, strategic, and engaging, the goals will lay forgotten like a rotting crop abandoned in the field.

The Bible also says in 2 Corinthians 9:6, "Whoever sows sparingly will also reap sparingly, and whoever sows generously will also reap generously." The idea of doing little, tiny things consistently over time is a powerful sentiment. It is one that we often overlook in our hurry to show spectacular results. Remember, educational leaders sometimes make snap decisions based on real-life pressures to have the answers instantly. That tendency is why this Leadership Cycle is so important when it comes to decision-making. Rarely are huge results evident immediately after action.

If a teacher one day decides to engage with students using nonconventional tools like tinkertoys, rap music, or maybe even food, I bet you the intended results will not appear on the first day. Colleagues may question those methods. Students will hopefully be delighted by the change but may be confused at first. It will take days, maybe even weeks, before the intended results arise. Three months down the line, the students are grasping concepts they struggled with before the different learning tools were introduced. That teacher found a way to ensure learning. and the method aligned beautifully with the school's vision.

The effect is so important, I'll say it once more: We don't get results from the big action we take in one day. We get results when we get the little things right the vast majority of the time, each and every day. Scott Ginsberg stated, "Consistency is far better than rare moments of greatness." Consistency, or lack thereof, can be the defining factor between failure or success. Without consistent effort, few people become experts. Without diligent practice, ballplayers do not improve. Without daily practice, musicians do not become virtuosos. Without consistent steps in the right direction that are aligned with the missions and vision, educational leaders impede transformation.

What happens when we're not consistent? Fear and mistrust are born. Those two powerful factors can dilute the impact of the vision. You, the leader, must maintain a consistent approach with your team. If you come in on Monday and reinforce the "fact" that establishing a new attendance policy is the utmost priority, and then the following week, after expectations have been clarified, allow three veteran teachers to arrive late without consequence, you've allowed cracks in your leadership foundation. Now your team doesn't know where they or the organizational priorities stand.

It does not stop there. Inconsistency kills ambition. If you, the leader, are inconsistent, then people will wait to act. They want to see what you are going to ask them to do first. They need to feel you out and determine which you they are dealing with on that particular day. They're using an act of self-preservation, which deadens empowerment and delays improvement. Instead of taking initiative, your people *wait and see.* Inconsistency creates a culture of reaction, and any area of inconsistency breeds opportunity for decay.

I see so many leaders who are fully aware of the importance of consistency, yet continue to struggle to establish a consistent mindset for a sustained period of time. Their lack of consistency is painful for all. Consistency creates progress in every aspect of our lives, but somehow, we continue to falter.

It is nothing short of tragedy that so many leaders find themselves consistent at one thing: starting something new. They can pilot a new project, spout off a new initiative, and get people excited about a new development. Then the leader stops before getting any results. Call it "shiny object syndrome," or just a penchant for starting new things, because starting and changing are "what leaders do."

The problem here is that such leaders are all too focused on the outcome rather than the process—they see that final result, and that is all that matters. Once the process is underway, it may take too much time, or leaders get sidetracked due to the overwhelming nature of multiple initiatives. Sometimes, a new, brilliant idea comes along, and progress stops. The leader encourages everyone to recalculate and begin at square one. Just like that, consistency is gone.

That is not to say that the outcome is unimportant. Nevertheless, if we become fixated on the outcome, it will work against us, no matter how compelling. Why? Because any outcome compelling enough to excite, motivate, and inspire is probably one that won't be achieved without hard work and sacrifice over a long period of time.

Without certain processes and systems in place to help us, most of us aren't able to maintain the effort needed to accomplish worthwhile outcomes. If you want to achieve your desired outcomes, you must build consistency into your plan, which is where the Leadership Cycle is so important. Do we follow through the Leadership Cycle? Or are we inconsistent because of time, urgency, or any number of the things that may distract us? If we follow through, then we can ensure consistency and buy-in over time.

We can put it into a simple equation:

Vision + Strategic Planning + Consistent Right Actions = Success

A leader develops a vision because he or she believes in a future. People can catch a vision and collaborate on the mini-missions needed to reach that vision. Their participation is fueled by passion and strategic planning, and it is consistent action, strategic planning, and vision that come together and lead to success.

But remember, it is your job to ensure clarity along the way.

Reflective Activity 6.2: "Consistent Impact"

Reflective Questions:

- What are three areas in which you are consistent?

- What impact is your consistency having on others?

- What are three areas in which you are inconsistent?

- What challenges or barriers are impeding your ability to be consistent?

- Identify one action step you can take today to minimize or eliminate a barrier to your consistency.

Key Points

- The first step in the Leadership Cycle for educational leaders is to ensure clarity of the mission.

- The burden of clarity always rests on the communicator, so refrain from using ambiguous words with multiple meanings.

- A great way to ensure clarity in a conversation is to ask your listener, "Would you mind sharing with me what you're taking away from our conversation?"

- The leader establishes the vision because he or she has a passion and motivation for the future.

- Missions are established collaboratively as long as they align with the vision.

- Buy-in can be achieved by engaging in an honest and transparent dialogue, breaking down large goals into smaller actionable steps, listening to others, obtaining and processing feedback, and communicating progress often and consistently.

- Consistency will make or break your ability to transform and cultivate change in your organization, and it starts with the leader.

CHAPTER 7 - STRATEGIC PLANNING AND DECISION-MAKING

"Always plan ahead. It wasn't raining when Noah built the ark."

— Howard Ruff

Let's digest the second step of the Leadership Cycle: Ensuring Strategic Planning and Decision-Making. It is a very complex step, but with a proper breakdown, you will begin to see the simplest elements make up the foundation of strategic planning. In fact, your personal definition of strategic planning will likely transform by the end of this chapter.

Strategic planning isn't taught in most schools. So, how can we expect our teachers to implement it in their own professional lives? As a leader, it is your responsibility to teach and emulate strategic planning. The good news is that it does not take more money to plan strategically. It is just a different level of thinking and processing. A pilot can still fly an aircraft safely even if they do not know the ADM thought process. However, risk is greatly reduced when they engage in a different level of thinking and follow the steps in order. Strategic planning is a lot like that. It is thinking about all the tiny steps that lead to the larger goal. All you need to do is engage the right people in a collaborative effort to strategically plan.

Of course, many companies fail to take strategic planning seriously. A 2005 report from *Harvard Business Review* found that 85% of executive leadership teams spend less than one hour per month discussing strategy, and that 50% spend no time at all discussing it! The same report also revealed that, on average, 95% of an organization's employees do not understand said organization's strategy.

Before we dive into the roots and fruits of strategic planning, consider this question: what are two things that are completely out of our control?

You may be able to curate an expansive list, but the two elements we are looking for in this case are *time* and *change*. Time and change are going to happen whether we want them to or not. Both are inevitable constructs of life that are inherently neutral. They are neither constructive nor destructive. They can be optimized, or they can victimize. But any perception or notion of control over time and change is simply an illusion.

A successful leader is defined by the way he or she manages time and change. After all, we become what we are as a result of how we use time and how we manage the change in our lives.

If an individual spends his or her time reading medical books and studying medicine, he or she is most likely going to be extremely knowledgeable and well versed in medical vernacular. He or she also will be inclined to add value to the medical profession as a doctor or nurse. If an individual spends his or her time practicing a musical instrument with vigor, commitment, and purpose, he or she will develop the skills of a master musician. However, if someone spends their time doing nothing, reading nothing, committed to nothing…well, you can probably guess what might become of them.

We really are defined by how we manage our time and the changes we encounter. In fact, time and change are so important that I call them *building blocks*. They are a commodity that every single living human being has in common. We all have the same 24 hours each day, and you become who you are based on how you use your 24.

In the previous chapter, we discussed fixed mindset and growth mindset. Anyone with a fixed mindset is going to use time and change as excuses to play the victim. "I don't have enough time," or "My circumstances changed and threw me off course, so I could not plan effectively." Although these reasons may be valid, they are also fixed statements. The growth-minded leader is optimistic about finding opportunities to maximize the use of time and change. The challenges that time and change present will excite the leader with a growth mindset.

There is a statement attributed to author Stephen Keaugue: "Proper planning and preparation prevents poor performance." If we take that saying and apply it to our educational systems, we can tackle multiple types of poor performance.

Proper planning and preparation prevents poor student performance, poor teacher performance, and poor institutional performance throughout the district or region, but many leaders take action without proper planning. Effective leaders plan ahead for lasting success because if you do not have a plan, you do not have a focus.

What Can Effective Leaders Control?

Born in 1848, Vilfredo Federico Damaso Pareto was an Italian civil engineer, philosopher, and sociologist, among other achievements. After determining that 80% of the land in Italy was owned by 20% of the population, Pareto coined the terms "vital few" and "trivial many." Their meaning is important because Pareto is credited with developing what is now known as the 80/20 rule. That is, 80% of results come from 20% of the action. Pareto's universal truth regarding the imbalance of inputs and outputs became immensely popular in time management, leadership development, and self-help books about healthy habits across the board.

As general examples of the 80/20 rule, if 80% of consequences occur from 20% of action, then, in generalized terms, 80% of crime is committed by 20% of the population; 80% of pollution comes from 20% of factories; 80% of a company's sales are generated by 20% of a company's customers.

Effective leaders face a paradox in their use of time. It always feels like there is not enough time to plan in a thorough, strategic, and collaborative way when faced with distractions and a lack of focus. Yet, they are expected to plan strategically as a core function of their job.

To overcome the 80/20 rule, leaders need to spend more time planning on the front end, spending more time to get their job done right in the first place, which will supercharge productivity. When we start talking about planning as well as strategy in planning, we need to remember that in every mission (and mini-mission) there is a goal.

The first step is to know specifically what you are trying to accomplish and what the impact will be. If you're going to be strategic, you have to think through the obstacles and anticipate them. You have to identify the knowledge, skills, and information you need to be successful. Then, once you've established these elements, you must identify the people whose help, support, and collaboration you will need.

That's a lot of preparation, and yet, there is more.

Once you have established what you want and what the goal is, you now have to determine all the steps needed to reach that goal. Every single step. Successful leaders plan each day, week, month, and sometimes year in advance. Such leaders are not reactive.

The first 20% of time you spend planning out your organizational goals will be worth 80% of the time and effort required to achieve that goal. Take 20% of your time to plan 80% of your month. Each minute spent on planning saves 10 minutes on execution.

There is a saying I have heard before that goes, "If you don't have time to do it right the first time, when will you have time to do it over?" Think about that statement for a moment. Effective leaders make time to get it right. They think through every element possible. They take the time on the front end so that they don't have to make time on the back end.

Effective leaders must take the time to be strategic. You have to look around corners and proactively anticipate what obstacles could be lurking at every turn. If you apply the 80/20 rule to your daily work, you will spend much less time having to rework your plan, review your plan, revamp your plan, rewind your plan, recover from mistakes made during inadequate planning, and more. Effective leaders minimize risk. They also minimize waste.

In the next section, let's explore the definition of strategic planning.

Reflective Activity 7.1: "Planning Time"

Reflective Questions:

- What percentage of your time is currently devoted to planning?

- What are three most influential adjustments you can make to your weekly schedule in order to increase the time you invest in strategic planning?

Redefining Strategic Planning

In education, the term "strategic planning" is a connotation for an outcome, but it is so far from that result in reality.

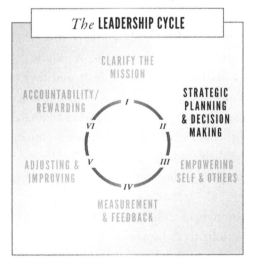

The **LEADERSHIP CYCLE**

Strategic planning is a process through and through. When leaders talk about definitions of strategy, most will say that a strategy is a plan. But it's not just any plan. It is vital we understand the difference for ourselves. Too many leaders are comfortable with their strategy. When you become comfortable with your strategy, there is a good chance that it isn't a good one. Effective leaders understand that a good strategy will stretch their comfort zones.

Planning and other activities will always dominate strategy unless a conscious effort is made to prevent it. Strategic planning is a blueprint for the work you will do to achieve your goal. Strategic thinking is the process that you take to get there—the practice of orienting decisions with the end goal in mind. Strategic thinking is the input to strategic planning. In short, it is foresight. Strategic thinkers resist the urge to let one decision dictate future decisions. Effective leaders accept that good strategy is not the product of hours of research, modeling, and developing the perfect conclusion. Instead, good strategy is achieved by simple and quite rough-and-ready processes of thinking about what it will take to achieve what you want. At the end of the day, it takes a lot of courage and determination, but leaders who use our strategic thinking and planning will drive proactive change.

Effective Leader Decision-Making

Strategy is implemented through decision. We know decisions are essential for change. Effective leaders are decisive, and they establish clear decision-making frameworks to help them navigate difficult choices. They anticipate and manage uncertainty. When we're talking about anticipating problems and challenges, effective leaders know it's important to engage in brainstorming on their own and collectively. Brainstorming allows leaders to identify prospective conditions or events that could negatively affect the mission.

Effective decision makers understand that they are not trying to be prophetic but are working to anticipate potential obstacles and manage them. It is not that you're going to get it all right or accurate all the time, but you will train yourself and your staff to think through potential obstacles—imagining what could happen, exploring a range of possibilities. Then, when the possibilities become reality, you and your team are prepared for the best and worst scenarios.

The second mark of effective decision makers is their ability to decipher when to rely on evidence and when to trust intuition. Most leaders believe their intelligence will always help them make the best decisions. In reality, they rely on their intelligence as a crutch when intuition is equally important in the decision-making progress.

The reason intuition is so important is that it is developed over a period of time. It is largely shaped by past experiences, past knowledge, professional encounters, and more. Of course, leaders should not rely solely on intuition. One extreme or another is never ideal. There should be a delicate balance between calling intelligence and/or intuition into play. Effective leaders make systemic decisions based on a combination of intuition and knowledge supported by data.

In short, evidence-based experiences guide intuition, and effective leaders rely on a combination of resources for strategic decision-making.

Emotional Intelligence

Effective leaders ensure that they can balance emotion and reason to make decisions that will benefit the organization, which is where Emotional Intelligence (EQ) comes into play.

EQ is the ability to understand your emotions as well as those of others. It is one of the most important qualities of an effective leader. In his book *Leadership: The Power of Emotional Intelligence,* Daniel Goleman states, "a leader's degree of emotional intelligence is directly related by how effective they are to motivate others, get them to commit, and get them in the best zone."

Effective leaders bring the best out of the people they work with. Goleman says, "Emotions are contagious." Naturally, a leader's emotions are contagious, so being a leader who is calm in the storm is vital. A leader's mood will resonate with others and can set the tone of the entire organization.

Most decisions that leaders have to make are crucial. They could be budgetary or personnel related. They could be about classroom policies or something incredibly high stakes that could make or break the organization. There is a reliance upon the leader to make swift, tough, influential, wide-ranging decisions. That pressure can evoke emotions of frustration, fear, anxiety, self-doubt, and even anger. If a leader is engaging in planning for their educational institution and is in a heightened sense of emotion, what kind of impact will that state of mind have on the people working within the organization?

Leaders do not have to be emotionless robots. I'm not suggesting they hide their feelings away. To deny an emotion is like cleaning up a room full of dirty clothes by hiding the clothes under the bed, in the closet, or under the rug. Sure, the room appears clean, but eventually, you will still have to deal with the mess you hid away. It is okay to experience emotions in the decision-making process, but effective leaders ensure that those emotions do not guide their decisions. If a leader makes emotional decisions or fails to rely on his or her own emotional intelligence before making a big decision, the driving emotions behind that decision will emanate throughout the organization.

Emotional Intelligence consists of self-awareness, self-management, social awareness, and relationship management, which are Goleman's four quadrants of EQ. They are essential for understanding the balance between emotions and decision-making (and the role emotions do play).

Self-awareness is the foundation of all aspects of Emotional Intelligence. It means you have the ability to recognize your own strengths, emotions, values, weaknesses, and drivers. It is the ability to understand your own impact on others.

Effective leaders recognize their emotions and understand how to separate emotional drivers from the decision-making process by identifying the root of the emotion and casting it aside so as not to cloud judgment. Let's say a leader gets in a fight with his or her spouse the morning before work. As they drive together to their office, they get stuck in traffic, making them rush to prepare for an early morning meeting. As the leader sits down to start the meeting, their morning has been full of emotions and even distractions. Someone could say something that triggers an emotional response, reminding the leader of the fight with their spouse. Yet, keen self-awareness is the superpower that helps the leader calmly facilitate the meeting and be fully present.

Self-management is the ability to control or redirect your disruptive emotions and adapt to changing circumstances in an optimistic way that keeps your team moving in a positive direction. Perhaps someone in this meeting says, "You seem as if you're rushed," to the leader. Rather than take offense to the observation, or jump into a defensive mode, the leader can take a deep breath and respond accordingly. "I appreciate your consideration. My commute took a little extra time from my preparation this morning, but I am glad to be here and am fully prepared to begin our meeting." That redirection aids the leader in managing his or her emotions, yet also drives the meeting in an optimistic direction.

Social awareness is the ability to put yourself in someone else's shoes and understand how they feel and react in certain situations. If a teacher is having a rough week or a student is really struggling with emotional management, social awareness gives the leader the lens to see from others' points of view and make decisions accordingly.

Relationship management is vital for leaders, as is relationship awareness. Awareness of your own distractions will help you foster meaningful relationships with your teachers and colleagues. To build trust, leaders must always manage relationships in order to forge new relationships and strengthen existing ones. Effective leaders do both by being genuine, decisive, transparent, and knowledgeable. The mastery of emotional intelligence is like a magnet, inviting others to trust the leader.

Roots and Fruits

Clearly, we shouldn't let emotions affect our decision-making process. Instead, with newfound awareness, you must identify your emotions and help others to do the same. Take time to recognize what you are feeling and trace that emotion to the root cause. Once you identify it and give yourself time to process that emotion, the intensity of the emotion will fade and you can move forward in a logical and productive manner. If you do not identify the root cause, you're in for a lot of wasted time and frustration.

Likewise, addressing the severity of problems is akin to addressing emotions. When planning, leaders who direct others to attack "easy" problems first might ignore the root issue. Imagine there was a fruit-bearing tree that had developed issues in the roots, and the leader knew it needed to be eliminated. The leader asked their teachers to take care of the problematic tree, but the teachers, seeing a great deal of fruit on the branches, decided to remove the fruit instead of investigating more thoroughly and removing the roots of this tree. They spent a great deal of time and effort solving what they thought was the problem, but guess what happened? The problematic tree was still there. The fruit grew back because the problem was only temporarily solved.

So often in leadership, we are conditioned to address the fruit. What is fruit in a school system? A student misbehaves—that is fruit. The teacher appears dysfunctional—that is fruit. The administrator is always turning in reports late—that is fruit. Each circumstance has a root cause.

At a particular middle school where I worked, the discipline left much to be desired. When assistant principals would walk to their office, they would be greeted by a line of students waiting to be addressed for disciplinary issues. The issues could be classroom misbehavior, fighting, dress code violation…you name it. The moment the assistant principals cleared the line of students, a new slew of misbehaving students came down the hall to their offices. It was a never-ending cycle.

Because of that issue, the assistant principals were unable to get into the classrooms, attend meetings, monitor the hallways, or do a range of responsibilities. They were always tied up addressing the line of misbehaviors. The teachers would get frustrated with the students and send them to the assistant principals for discipline. The principals would dole out disciplinary actions and send the students on their way (be it to in-school suspension, out-of-school suspension, or another disciplinary measure).

The constant revolving door-like process did not contribute to a productive or enjoyable environment. The teachers didn't appreciate having to stop their curricular activities to address the misbehaviors. The assistant principals felt ineffective because they couldn't attend to their other duties, which quite possibly could prevent some of the misbehaviors from occurring. Most of all, the students were not happy. They didn't feel as if they belonged. They didn't feel successful. They didn't feel motivated. There was a lot of leaf picking and fruit picking of the tree at this school. With every pick, something grew back. Progress went backward. Something had to be done.

The principal made the controversial decision to spend the majority of his time, energy, and effort working to identify and address the root issues causing the majority of the "fruit" problems. The administration engaged in strategic planning for how they would identify the 20% of the teachers experiencing—and in some cases, causing—80% of the issues. They would work collectively on an aligned approach to provide targeted support, training, development, and progress monitoring to ensure improvement. That approach meant that there would be short-term, temporary sacrifices in order to focus on long-term, sustainable results. Students sent down for discipline would have to be sent back to class. Attempts to reduce recidivism weren't even working with discipline, so it shouldn't have been much of a sacrifice. Yes, some teachers would be upset; however, the administrators would help them understand and manage such changes for the greater good.

If the administration could get into the classrooms more frequently and identify the challenges before they escalated, they could work with the teachers to develop strategies to get the kids feeling motivated, engaged, valued, and desirous to be successful.

In addition, what happens when the administration spends more time in the classroom, hallways, and cafeterias, meeting with and talking with students and teachers? The presence of the administrators is a proactive deterrent to off-task behavior for both teachers and students. The administrators' visibility, participation, and collaborative efforts have a positive impact on the culture and climate. The administrators are able to gain a more in-depth understanding of exact issues and build stronger connections to support improvement.

Their attention identified the root. And by supporting improvement in just a few teachers who directly contributed to a challenging environment for students, spending 20% of time working on the root solved 80% of the issues.

What was the root? Students were misbehaving and requiring discipline because they were not engaged with the learning. Bored students wanted attention. They were seeking connection and felt that acting out was a way to achieve it. When students are not engaged and not understanding the lesson at hand, there is no relationship with the teacher and no connection to the learning environment.

With their discovery in hand, the assistant principals worked with teachers on the technical aspects of engagement and alignment as well as the adaptive aspects to motivate, engage, and empower both the teachers and learners. Those teachers needed the resources to determine how to handle behavioral situations *before* they occurred instead of dealing with the issues *after* the disruption.

Even technical actions such as greeting each student at the door and checking in on their mood had a huge impact at the root level, minimizing the fruit. And by supporting improvement in just one teacher who had a direct correlation to student achievement, spending 20% of time working on the root solved 80% of the issues. The root was there all along. It just needed to be uncovered.

If leaders start to embrace a mindset of identifying the root cause of an issue, instead of picking at the problem, there would be more sustainability in the results and in achievements.

Strategic planning falls under the umbrella of how we approach issues and problems as well as the thinking that it takes. In the long term, you develop teachers who have the skills, mindset, resources, tools, and perspective that drastically minimize the fruit-bearing activities.

Reflective Activity 7.2: "Root Cause Analysis"

Reflect on a current issue you are experiencing, its likely root cause, and possible solutions.

Issue		Likely Root Cause		
Description	Impact on Student Learning	Description	Adaptive Challenges	Technical Challenges

Possible Solutions		
Description	Risks	Measure of Success

Seven Principles of Planning Strategically

As you've grasped the difference between roots and fruits, here is a helpful summary of best practices to consider when planning in a strategic nature. These principles should be top of mind as you ensure that the missions of your organization come to fruition.

1. **Avoid Planning for the Sake of Planning.**

Some leaders and organizations engage in planning just to say they have planned. Look at any job description of an educational leader, and you will find a section on "engage and develop strategic plans"—but that's not what they're really doing.

When you plan for the sake of planning, you're going to get out exactly what you put into it. If you've been enlightened by anything in this chapter, may it be that if you are going to take the time to do it, you take the time to do it right. There is a lot of preparation and development that must occur before a strategic plan is signed, sealed, and delivered. Strategic plans are powerful guides that can pave the road for lasting, positive change. Put all your effort into the front end so you can see back-end results.

2. **Plan for Impact.**

Any time a leader is planning, they should always be focused on impact. Their vision must inspire the planning teams to pay attention to changes in the culture and climate. Everyone involved needs to pay attention to the adaptive and technical aspects of the planning process. What can be solved by an expert? What requires relationship building and trust? Leaders must set meaningful priorities to pursue results. Plan for impact, not just to check a box.

3. **Invite the Right Team.**

Effective leaders get the right people involved. Those charged with the execution of the plan should be involved at the onset. You don't want to do things *to* people. You want to do things *with* people. As a leader, you must champion those involved in planning and champion to keep everyone on track. The right team is filled with the right motivation and desire to get things done to benefit the greater good.

4. **Monitor Consistently.**

Effective leaders monitor consistently. Most plans that are developed are created, talked about, and then forgotten. They lie collecting dust in a filing folder, a binder, or perhaps never make the transition from the digital word processor onto physical paper. To be effective, plans must be used and reviewed continually. People change, circumstances change, and priorities may even change. How can a strategic plan developed at the beginning of the school year address the issues that have arisen during the second half of the school year? (Granted, if the leaders anticipated potential roadblocks, those issues may indeed be in the plan). The strategic plans should be seen as living, breathing documents that can change when needed. The plan must also live in the minds, hearts, and beliefs of those in charge of executing that plan. For that outcome to happen, the plan should be top of mind.

5. **The Best Plans Are Flexible**

Along with monitoring consistently, there should be a generous allowance of flexibility. Although the strategic nature of the plan is to look around corners and identify potential challenges, plans have to be nimble and adaptive to all the nuances and changes that come with working with and leading people. Effective leaders understand that. Those aspects are part of the strategic nature of plans as most must be malleable to make long-lasting change.

6. **Establish a Culture of Accountability**

Just as the first principle is never to plan for the sake of planning, effective leaders must establish a culture of accountability and follow through with it. They must be resolute once a plan is developed and resources are deployed for the delivery of strategy. When there is not a successful delivery or strategy, effective leaders reflect on their part of ensuring clarity, support and resources, and take the necessary steps to hold people accountable if and when the results do not come to fruition. The culture of accountability is achieved by ensuring clarity of the mission, continual monitoring of the plans, and a focus on impacts.

7. **Focus**

Effective leaders avoid a lack of focus. As we said before, when leaders do not have a road map or let distractions affect their ability to plan strategically, there will be cracks in the foundation of that strategic plan. Effective leaders avoid wasting resources and time. They've spent so much time on the front end by preserving the stewardship of resources that such leaders have effectively not wasted their own time or the resources of the organization. Effective leaders understand that strategically developed plans must be focused and include a manageable number of goals, objectives, and initiatives. Although the planning is strategic in nature, fewer tactics in focus are better than numerous and nebulous ones.

Reflective Activity 7.3: "Strategic Planning"

When it comes to ensuring a quality strategic-planning process, asking reflective questions are key. Consider the questions below as you reflect on your own strategic planning.

Reflective Questions:

- What specific two or three objectives are we planning to accomplish?
- What impact will our objective(s) have on student learning?
- How will we measure success with each objective?
- Who owns each objective? Who will lead the efforts to ensure results?
- How will we know we have the right people involved in the process?

Key Points

- Two things that are out of everyone's control are time and change.
- The 80/20 rule states that 20% of action yields 80% of consequence. You can manage your time by adopting the 80/20 rule into your daily life to supercharge your productivity.
- Strategy is implemented through decision.

- Effective leaders have focus and do not let distractions or emotions affect decision-making processes.

- Effective leaders anticipate roadblocks and check around corners when planning strategically.

- Emotional Intelligence (EQ) is the ability to understand your emotions as well as those of others. It is one of the most important qualities of an effective leader.

- When addressing any issue, any problem, or any emotion, it is paramount to determine the root cause. If you tackle the fruit of the issue, it will always grow back. You must address the roots for lasting change.

CHAPTER 8 - EMPOWERMENT OF SELF AND OTHERS

"The beauty of empowering another human
being is that we never lose our own power in the process."

— Barbara Coloroso

In the 2016 Summer Olympic Games, the U.S. female track-and-field relay team competed in the 4×100 meter relay. The star-studded team consisted of Tianna Bartoletta, Allyson Felix, English Gardner, and Tori Bowie. All eyes were on them in hopes of their defending the U.S. gold title from the 2012 London Olympic Games.

In the qualifier heat, these four women were prepared to earn their spot in the championship relay. Bartoletta, Felix, Gardner, and Bowie had trained hard for that moment. The four women ate to fuel their bodies and made countless sacrifices to compete on the world's biggest athletic stage. Each competitor put in thousands of hours of training individually and as a team. There was a lot of pressure for the defending champions, and a lot of expectations rode on their shoulders.

At the sound of the gun, Bartoletta shot off the block to get a strong lead for her team. Felix held her arm behind her back, eager to receive the baton from Bartoletta. If you watch a relay race closely, you will see that the runners rarely look at their teammates delivering the baton. Instead their eyes are forward, and they trust their teammate to get the baton in their hand.

After a clean handoff, Felix took off. She made her way around the track and approached Gardner, who like Felix before, awaited the baton. But something wasn't right. A runner from the Brazilian team bumped Felix's arm, and she dropped the baton onto the track. It was a relay athlete's worst nightmare come true.

But they would learn the importance of empowerment that day. As we'll see, they returned from the brink and kissed the stars.

Leadership is like a relay race, where the baton is a baton of empowerment.

You see, it is one thing to develop a plan strategically, but it is an entirely different thing to empower others to follow through with the plan. The latter is why the next step in the Leadership Cycle is Empowering Self and Others. It only makes sense to empower people after a plan has been decided, and feedback can only be fair and effective after your people are empowered.

What do we mean by empower? For our purposes, to empower is the process of encouraging and stimulating an individual to think, behave, and make decisions toward the mission. Empowerment is permission to take a proactive approach to learning and experiencing what is currently, or will eventually, affect yourself and others.

By now, you've ensured clarity of the vision and mission. You're well versed in planning strategically. Instead of having employees ask permission or wait for direction, the effective leader empowers them to become more responsible and accountable as a result of self-direction. Empowered people add value to the mission. They have the ability to change the culture and climate of an organization from one of reactivity to one of proactivity. Empowered people do not wait for change to affect them. They initiate change to influence results.

Two Focus Areas of Empowerment

Effective leaders must focus primarily on two different perspectives of empowerment. The first is a focus on self-empowerment.

Sounds easy, but what does it really mean? A leader's job is to take the necessary steps to gain proper insight and understanding to ensure that they have the knowledge required to empower others. You can't teach what you don't know—and you can't provide an experience for others if you have not experienced it yourself.

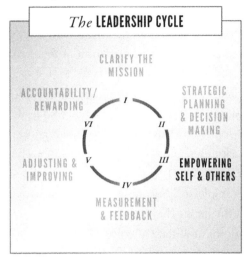

Self-empowerment, in the context of the Leadership Cycle, is the process of gaining that insight and understanding to empower others. It is possible to inform and plan at a surface level of understanding but not be empowering. The goal of empowering yourself is to maximize your potential and everyone else's.

Effective principals build up their teachers, provide those teachers with the resources for them to learn from, help teachers realize their leadership potential, and then trust those very same teachers to do their work. As a leader, if you attempt to solve everyone's problems, you will eventually burn out. You will create an atmosphere of dependency on your availability and reliance on your knowledge. If everything revolves around your decision-making, you could be missing out on the creativity, experiences, and collective wisdom of great contributors. But if you can establish a culture of proactive consumers of information, the momentum you will build and the time you will save will be instrumental in achieving a greater level of success in a more timely manner.

Empowerment in leadership is like a relay race—not a sprint. Leadership is not just about how fast you run your leg, but about how effectively you pass the baton to the next runner so they can run their leg of the race. You are not successful in a relay alone. The whole team wins, but the key to the win is a successful passing of the baton in the exchange or "empowerment" zone.

Effective leaders model a mindset of continuous improvement. They are constantly leading the learning. Self-empowered leaders are never satisfied with surface-level knowledge. Effective leaders constantly analyze their strengths and weaknesses, and they foster a continuous hunger for learning and growth.

Here is an example to illustrate self-empowerment. Let's say there is a room full of principals. They are hearing for the first time from their district leadership that the state will unveil a new system for teacher evaluations for the upcoming year. The way they have been done for years will be optimized and will change. In fact, to prepare for the change, the state has rolled out trainings on the new system along with evaluation templates for principals to get familiar with.

The principals are halfway through the current school year. They know the current system backward and forward. In fact, they could evaluate teachers in their sleep! Why bother taking time out of their busy days to poke around the new system? They can learn it when it is time to use it.

That approach is a complete and utter lack of self-empowerment. When the new system replaces the old, these principals will become victims of change. If they're focused on the old way and not learning the new way, they will become frustrated and look for excuses as to why they are failing at implementing the new system in a way that yields the desired results.

Instead, self-empowered principals find small chunks of time to get to know the new system. They take the time to strategically review the old evaluation and compare it to the new one, observing similarities and differences, and begin to think through potential obstacles and challenges with implementation as well as to start formulating ideas and plans to overcome those challenges. If they wait for someone to direct and guide them, their response will be purely reactive when the time comes.

Self-empowered leaders are also proactive. They take advantage of everything available to them so that when the change comes, they've practiced and are prepared for that very moment. And remember, leaders are models in the organization, so if leaders are not engaging in self-empowerment, they are also creating a culture of;

- "I'll know it once I'm informed."

- "I'll do it once I'm directed."

- "I'll understand it once I'm taught."

- "I'll pay attention once it becomes important."

That mindset is dangerous because a reactive approach breeds an attitude of dependence. When you are depending on others to show you the way, you're putting accountability on everything and everyone but yourself.

That is how rumors start. That is how frustrations are born. That is what encourages fixed mindsets. Reactive people gather together and complain, "This school doesn't care about teachers," or "This school doesn't invest in students," or any other statements that blame the organization at large. Reactive people are often bred in a culture of dependence, and a culture of dependence stems from lack of empowerment. To empower yourself means you are a proactive consumer of information, not a reactive recipient.

When leaders engage in self-empowerment, they demonstrate the priority of a growth mindset by leading the learning. Their modeling is a powerful way to ensure that a growth mindset permeates throughout an organization. Effective leaders establish credibility by learning and engaging in the discussion of a deeper level of understanding and by building trust.

I'll say it again: Leadership is a team sport, and there is no weakness in demonstrating a growth mindset. Their participation will foster trust throughout the organization. Finally, when a leader engages in self-empowerment, they minimize the chance of being victimized by someone else's timeline. When you know what is coming, you can prepare for it.

Leaders are always learners. They're always learning about what they are accountable and responsible for.

Empowerment of Others

When we start talking about empowering others, oftentimes many people think to empower is to inform. Information is a part of empowerment, but it is not the only part. Empowerment stems far beyond information.

To empower is to provide information and experience. People can have information, but the experience is what fosters beliefs. And beliefs shape actions, whereas actions produce results. You can't read a dissertation and say, "Oh, I'm empowered." A leader can't hand teachers a binder and say, "You'll be empowered after reading this." They will be informed, not empowered. Effective leaders have to think about how to provide experiences to engage with the information. Information and experience are what foster empowerment.

We learn by experience. Imagine if I tried to teach you how to tie a bowline knot by reading the instructions aloud to you. Would you be able to translate that information and tie the knot? Maybe. However, if you and I practiced tying the knot together, and I walked you through each step after demonstrating the knot, would you pick up the practice faster? Yes, because I provided you with an experience to use the information I wanted to relay. Providing information is helpful and will inform, but providing an experience based on that information is more helpful and will *transform*. Moreover, people feel empowered when they have what they need to solve their own problems, which simultaneously frees up time for leaders to address bigger and more macro-level issues.

Need proof? An *Employee Job Satisfaction and Engagement Study* conducted by the Society for Human Resource Management (SHRM) in 2016 found that "70% of employees rank being empowered to take action as an important action of engagement." When people have the knowledge to do their jobs, they feel good. Add on authorization to do their jobs along with resources, and they feel even better. So, how do effective leaders empower others?

1. Effective leaders empower others by delegating to them.

Such leaders share, appropriately, organizational authority. Now, "sharing" doesn't mean the leader dumps busywork onto subordinates or gives away tasks he or she does not enjoy doing. That's not empowerment. When the leader delegates tasks of importance, though, others feel empowered. They feel the leader trusts them.

In turn, the leader is providing opportunities for innovation, creativity, and an increase in morale. Everyone has a stake in the mission, and delegation solidifies that sentiment. It is also important to note that we cannot confuse empowerment with abandonment. When we say "empower people," it doesn't mean empower them, provide them with information and experiences, then leave. Information and experience are not a replacement for the leader. They are supplementals. Empowerment is very much collaborative in nature with the leader leading the learning effort and delegating appropriately.

2. Effective leaders empower others by educating them.

The growth and development of people is a vital priority in effective leadership. Part of that comes through educating. Effective leaders are also effective teachers. It is not about giving information—it is about ensuring clarity and giving experiences and opportunities to engage in that information.

3. Effective leaders empower others by encouraging them.

Courage is a special type of power. It is a mental strength to face fear and step outside the box. Many effective leaders are masters in the art of inspiration. They have the right words to lift someone up when they have fallen. They have the right lesson to share when someone has failed. Those talents can be life changing and empowering. But they must be genuine and personal. Personal encouragement is far more influential than a generalized complimentary statement.

4. Effective leaders empower others by providing experiences that allow others to engage in the knowledge.

How often do we see teachers hired as assistant principals and immediately realize they might not have been as prepared as even they originally thought? They look great on paper and passed all their certifications, but when they get into that role, all that theory, all that information now has to be put in practice.

Look at medical students. They start as interns and slowly gain more responsibility as their knowledge and experience accumulates. However, this type of experiential training is not often the case with educational leaders. If a teacher turned assistant principal hasn't experienced being cursed out by a parent with a line of students waiting out the door as the phone rings and the email notification dings like there is a fire, then have they really been empowered by their background?

The same can be said for principals. Many were former assistant principals. Now they're heads of the school and in charge of the school's budget. Sure, they may have seen the budget, but have they had the opportunity to practice allocating funds, identify academic priorities for financial alignment, deal with district pressures, and get stakeholders on the same page?

Those examples show why it is so important for leaders to empower others and offer experiences in addition to the knowledge. Knowledge is necessary, but experience is required to practice and use that knowledge to be empowered and successful.

Reflective Activity 8.1: "Empowerment"

When it comes to ensuring empowerment of others, consider these questions:

Reflective Questions:

Information

- In what ways am I preparing myself beyond surface-level knowledge of the information?

- In what ways is information being shared with others? Are those ways conducive to how people best absorb information?

Experiences

- What practical experiences are being provided to engage with the information in a meaningful way?

- What potential for failure is being provided?

- What lessons are being learned through failure?

- How am I working with others?

Feedback

- How regularly am I providing quality feedback?

- How am I measuring the quality of my feedback?

- What systems have been established for me to obtain transparent, honest, timely, and meaningful feedback?

- How am I responding to, acting on, and communicating adjustments or improvements based on received feedback?

Impact without Imposition

Some leaders will try to impose their will and beliefs onto the people they lead. That is not empowerment. Effective leaders understand that empowerment is not about imposition, but it is about influence. In order to understand the importance of having an impact without imposition, though, we must first understand the dynamics of influence on empowerment.

The beliefs of an effective leader come out in their principles and behavior. They lead in learning, go the extra mile, practice consistency, and believe in the best of other people. When working with others, effective leaders provide opportunities and experiences to move people toward what is best for the organization. Sometimes, that momentum means leading people out of their comfort zone. Improvement isn't always comfortable. To motivate and inspire others to move into a realm of discomfort, effective leaders require influence. Influence is more important than power.

Power demands, but influence suggests. Power is forced, but influence is voluntary. Power is a one-way dialogue, but influence creates conversation. Power leads to an increasingly disengaged organization, but influence boosts employee retention, engagement, and morale.

Why Some Leaders Refrain from Empowering

Why would a leader refrain from empowering others? Isn't the whole goal of leadership to empower, inspire, and mold future leaders to continue an evolution of transformation?

There are many reasons. The first is the obvious scapegoat: a lack of time. Leaders are pulled in many different directions and can easily become victims of their time. It is so much easier to give someone something to read than to provide an experience for empowerment. The latter is much more effective, but the first one checks the box.

The second reason is more sinister. Unfortunately, from time to time, leaders are hesitant to empower because they are insecure. When your self-worth is tied so closely to your title, you're going to protect both at all costs. Those types of leaders never want to leave their positions because they have tied their position to their identity. Their self-worth is so intertwined with their leadership role that they want no change, no challenge, and no one to take their place. That insecurity gives way to selfishness, and those leaders are only interested in their own ambition rather than the development of others.

Insecurity is why people will fight to stay in positions and fail to share information. They will refrain from investing everything they have. Not only do these leaders fail to produce leaders, they also make sure there are no empowered leaders around them. Ineffective leaders do not want anyone around them who will compete with them or challenge them.

Effective leaders understand the need for challenging discourse and other perspectives. They welcome fresh ideas and are not offended by questions or the need for justification. They understand that from time to time there will be nonconformists in the organization who question everything.

Ineffective leaders dismiss such nonconformists and do their best to keep them informed but not empowered. It's a crucial mistake.

Effective leaders understand that nonconformists will question the system because the established system isn't working anymore. Effective leaders understand that they have blind spots, and it is often the nonconformist who will have the gall to help the leader identify where those blind spots are. Nonconformists provide new ideas that break up old traditions. Ineffective leaders feel secure in old traditions, since those traditions protect their positions.

Be careful to understand that empowerment is not the same as entitlement—which is the greatest weakness in leadership. People who feel entitled think that benefits, privileges, and results should come automatically. Leaders who feel entitled feel that everything is everyone else's fault. Leaders who are empowered, on the other hand, are humble. They make sure the people who gave them power are not let down. Ineffective leaders put paperwork before people work.

Yet, the goal of leadership is to help others discover their potential. Effective leaders pass the baton in such a way that they collectively and collaboratively run the race together. Effective leaders are not afraid of empowering others, including nonconformists, because they understand the dynamic of the race. They are focused both on the short- and long-term success of the individuals and the organization. They realize they could be here today and gone tomorrow. They do not want the people or the organization to suffer in their absence. Remember Martin Luther King Jr., who had a dream but said he may not be around to see it. That's the mindset of effective leaders. They have a vision, and even if they're not around to see it come to fruition, they have empowered others to step up and be leaders and carriers of the vision.

Effective educational leaders know that their role is not about them. Everything they do is for the students, the teachers, the organization, and the community. Effective leaders don't want an organization with a leader. They want an organization full of leaders.

The Relay Race

It's important to say again: Leadership is a relay race of empowerment. When you observe a relay race, each person has their individual training that they do on their own. Maybe it is sprints, or practicing the push off the blocks, or timing strides and turnover rates. The individual athlete watches what they eat and drink, and is cognizant of their individual actions because they know it can affect the team. Once the individual training and preparation is complete, the racers come together as a team. They display team preparation, team commitment, team practice, unity, and a clear and unified mission.

When asked what is the most important part of a relay race, many people think it is the running. After all, they think, the fastest team wins! Running fast is important, but it is not the most important part.

The most important part of a relay race is the passing of the baton in a small area called the "exchange zone." It won't matter if an individual runner is the fastest in a leg if they miscalculate the handoff or violate that exchange zone. All the training, commitment, and hours of preparation would feel as if it were for nothing.

That is exactly how the women's 4×100 relay team felt on that fateful day in Rio. English Gardner picked up the baton and ran it to the next point. Despite disqualification, the women finished their race. They appealed their disqualification, citing interference from the competing team. After a review, the women won their appeal and were given a special heat to qualify for the championship relay. They would run on an empty track. There would be no excuses for a failed baton pass or error. Fortunately, they ran the fastest qualifying time without incident and were off to the finals.

But the story didn't end there. Right before the momentous championship meet, English Gardner realized she did not have her cleats. Felix gave her a backup pair, despite the size being off. The team could have viewed the situation as another setback and gone in with a disempowered attitude. Instead, they empowered each other. They had come this far and faced some pretty bizarre adversity. The U.S. team went on to win back-to-back gold medals in the 4×100 meter relay, successfully defending their championship.

In the context of leadership and empowerment, every mission is a relay race. The most important part is not how fast the leader runs, but how well they hand off the baton and what happens next. In fact, a good team has "spares"—substitutes who are trained to step in to play at any point and time for their particular role in the race.

After the handing of the baton, the runner doesn't simply turn his or her back on their teammate and walk away. Instead, they observe, focus, and encourage their teammate to run fast and exchange smoothly. When you watch a relay race, it is amazing how much trust the runners have in one another. The only way the team can win is if everyone empowers one another.

Imagine you have a runner who says, "I'm faster than all of you. I can do this all myself." Sure, they may be fast, but there is nothing like a fresh set of legs and lungs ready to sprint after a handoff. The egotistical solo runner will grow tired and weary. You can't outpace the collective ideas, efficacy, and brainchild of multiple leaders.

You want those fresh "legs" and "lungs" on your team. A lot of leaders disqualify themselves because they think they are in a solo race. They may not like or trust the team they have, but the end result will be a better likelihood of success.

Key Points

- To empower is the process of encouraging and stimulating an individual to think, behave, and make decisions toward the mission.

- Empowerment is taking a proactive approach to learning and experiencing what is currently or will eventually affect yourself and others.

- There are two types of empowerment: (1) self-empowerment (the process of gaining that insight and understanding to empower others), and (2) empowerment of others (the process of providing information and experiences to enhance, engage, educate, and inspire others to take action).

- Some leaders fail to empower others due to insecurity, tying their position to self-worth, or fear of competition.

- Empowerment is not the same as entitlement.

- Leadership is like a relay race, and the most important part is the handoff.

CHAPTER 9 - MEASUREMENT AND FEEDBACK

"The volume of your impacts is measured by the
direction of your movements, the passion with which you
inspire and the attitudes by which you make an influence!"

— Israelmore Ayivor

About 14 years ago, a good friend of mine had an idea that we should rent motorcycles and take a road trip from Dallas, Texas, to New York City. It would be a 10-day round trip, and everything we needed to survive would have to fit on the bikes.

I was teaching eighth grade U.S. History at the time, and thought I could use the road trip as an experience to highlight what students were learning about the 13 colonies. I planned on collecting memorabilia from the trip and sharing it with my students when we returned. We packed 10 days' worth of clothes and resources and hopped onto our 2007 Harley-Davidson Road Kings full of vigor, optimism, and a bit of naivety.

Now, weeks prior to the trip, my friend and I strategically planned our route and even mapped out contingency routes in case of unforeseen hazardous road conditions. Our goal was to avoid major highways as much as possible to witness the serene beauty of each county and town that the states had to offer. Seeing as how the 2007 Road Kings did not come equipped with technology such as GPS and navigational resources found on today's modern bikes, we had to rely on the accuracy of the good old-fashioned 16 × 12-inch *Rand McNally Road Atlas* map. My friend had an innate sense of direction that eludes me to this day. Therefore, his responsibility was handling our daily briefings regarding the route and weather. My responsibility was handling the bike maintenance and identifying the safest places for us to rest.

There is something to be said for the thrill, excitement, and adrenaline that comes with being on the open road. On the second day of our trip to New York, I felt inspired. Although we had already agreed on roles and responsibilities, I wanted to handle the daily briefing that day. I woke up early, got the bikes ready, and shared the itinerary with my buddy. This time, I would take the lead and handle our stops and exits.

We must have ridden for nine hours. As the sun set and we rode in the darkness, things felt a bit odd. Remember, we didn't have GPS on the bikes, and our phones did not have reception at the time. As we approached our 10th hour, I pulled us over to check the map. Well, where we were did not seem to be on the map at all. My friend trusted me. After all, my enthusiasm really won him over to take the lead for day two. That is, until his directional intuition kicked in.

"Sam, are we headed in the right direction?" he asked.

"Yeah, we are," I responded confidently.

At the next little town, he suggested we pull over and find the town on the map.

Well, turns out we had been going in the wrong direction for over an hour. We were far from home, limited with what we had for energy and resources. We did not have the means to be driving in the wrong direction for an entire hour. We were headed south when we needed to head north. I really messed up.

I was monitoring our movement, but I wasn't measuring it. Just because you are moving doesn't mean you're moving in the right direction. My inability to understand where we were was going cost us valuable time and resources. Now, we did get on the right path and eventually made it to our destination safely. I'm proud to say my friend and I have successfully navigated the country on four motorcycle road trips since then, with destinations ranging from Alaska to Nova Scotia—but the point of this story is that movement doesn't always mean progress. You need to measure your progress for movement to be *productive*. That's where measurement and feedback come into play.

Defining Measurement and Monitoring

That step is so incredibly important, because without providing timely and concise feedback, and without establishing a system to monitor and measure that feedback, you cannot go on to the next step in the leadership cycle. It all falls apart. How can you adjust and improve if you do not know how effective your feedback is? There is no blueprint to follow. There is no baseline for growth.

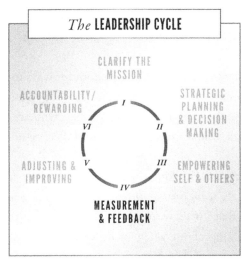

When you think of the terms "measurement" and "monitoring," how often are they used interchangeably? The answer is: often. The fact is, measurement and monitoring have very different meanings, especially for our purposes in education and leadership.

To monitor is to determine the status of an activity. Monitoring typically entails critically observing an activity or process. You can monitor a classroom lesson or students' progression of a classroom experiment, but monitoring in this sense may not involve specific measurements of quality or impact.

Measurement is a process used to determine value. If a leader is monitoring teaching, they're looking at the teaching. If a leader is measuring teaching, they are concerned with the value, quality, and specific evidence of learning. Measurement is a subset of monitoring and involves specific parameters.

Their difference is paramount because, in the Leadership Cycle, you don't monitor continuous improvement. You *measure* continuous improvement. You look for evidence of impact. Effective leaders understand the principle of quality versus quantity. In fact, effective leaders are nearly obsessed with this question: What is the evidence that this decision, this activity, this system is having the intended impact? Or this question: What is the evidence that this lesson is in alignment with what students need to ensure learning?

Effective leaders are always on the lookout for ways to measure impact, so one of the worst mistakes a leader can make is to assume. If ineffective leaders make assumptions about team members who are new to the organization, untested, unmonitored, or even unskilled, results and impact can be stunted.

Now, you may be thinking, *Well, if the ineffective leader assumes the new members of the team can't do their job, then morale and trust are out the window.* While that's true, we're not talking about negative assumptions, per se. We're talking about when ineffective leaders assume that since a new addition has great character, a strong intellect, and passion for their profession, they can be handed a map and sent on their way. Sure, the new person looks great on paper, but having great attributes doesn't mean the leader can forgo measurement of impact and feedback. Unless the leader checks in regularly to ensure the person is clear about the mission, is on track, has the resources and supports they need, and provides quality feedback, it is likely they will see unexpected and often disappointing results.

So, leaders cannot assume everyone knows what they are doing and are striving for excellence. Leaders must monitor and determine evidence of such, in addition to providing quality feedback for improvement. If you are the recipient of quality feedback, it means you are valued. Effective leaders do not assume. Instead, they develop systems to ensure the measurement of quality. They use those systems to glean knowledge so that they themselves, and others, can make wise choices.

Effective leaders do not want to waste their time, energy, or effort, especially because time is one of those resources we have a finite amount of. Therefore, effective leaders accomplish goals and get missions completed by and through people. They inspect what they expect. A positive and effective measurement process is a thoughtful and strategic activity designed to assess how closely key expectations are being fulfilled, ensure continued alignment, provide needed support, reinforce progress, and promote learning.

Skipping the Steps

Those are a lot of benchmarks for a positive and effective measurement process. Even the most seasoned strategic thinkers and planners may feel overwhelmed by that list. Indeed, out of all the steps on the Leadership Cycle, assessing progress is the step most neglected. There are a number of reasons:

1. *A Lack of Time and Attention*

"I just don't have the time to give everyone feedback."

"I don't have time to follow through on the feedback I give."

"I provided feedback, and I hope they take it to heart."

Effective leaders understand that whatever you allow, you cannot complain about. That's why developing those systems that measure what is critical to the organization is so important to effective leaders. Measurement and feedback are not "check the box" actions. They are vital tools that can transform an educational institution once everyone is on the same page and working toward a common mission.

How many schools out there could say that student discipline is a challenge? Well, effective leaders will establish clear end goals in order to face that challenge. Yes, that action takes time and attention, but it is immensely influential. Here's an example:

Let's say that discipline is a challenge for a school. An effective leader will review trend data for the past three to five years on teachers, grade levels, cohort groups, time of day of most frequent occurrences of discipline, and more. That effort is where the knowledge-gathering comes into play. They won't assume they know why discipline is an issue (even though they may have some intuitive ideas). Instead, they will review the data for trends. But they won't stop there! They will take the data and ensure everyone in the organization is aware of the key findings. The effective leader will engage in dialogue about the impact that the data has on student and staff morale. They will investigate the data for impacts on workload for teachers, administration, and ultimately student achievement.

Together, as a team, everyone establishes one goal to determine where discipline markers should be each month, each semester, and at the end of the year. The right people are engaged in the strategic planning and decision-making process to determine the method of "root" intervention. That's right—there will be no fruit picking in this scenario. Campus leaders are empowered to engage in the development and support of the root intervention process.

Each month, the campus leaders report back to our effective leader on the impact of their support on student discipline. Together, they review the data and highlight what is working, what needs to be improved, and what needs to be adjusted. They discuss their measurement and obtain feedback from everyone. Together, everyone established a system where they could have a comprehensive understanding of exactly what is happening in the school related to discipline within the scope of a few meetings and some research.

No decisions were made unilaterally. No assumptions were made. The root interventions made discipline much less of a challenge for the school and enriched the student experience. What if we took the same system and process and applied them to everything else that needs to be measured in the educational realm? Some examples would be classroom observations, quality of professional learning communities, and reducing student tardiness with evidence of impact, to name a few.

2. *Monitoring, Measuring, and Micromanagement*

The second reason that leaders may skip the step of measuring progress in the Leadership Cycle is that they do not want to give others the impression they are micromanaging them. Checking in and providing feedback can often be misconstrued as helicopter leadership (like helicopter parenting but worse).

But effective leaders nip that preconceived notion in the bud straight away. The difference between micromanaging and measuring success is the perception of intent. If people see a leader checking in with a genuine attitude, with genuine interest in the work being done, and in a supportive instead of critical demeanor, they see that monitoring as a measurement of success.

On the other hand, if people see a leader coming in to criticize, demand, direct, berate, and hold accountable, they will perceive it as micromanaging. There is no trust, no belief, no empowerment.

3. *Lack of Metrics to Track Improvement*

When leaders do not establish clear metrics, clear benchmarks to track improvement, then ensuring measurement and feedback is an "easy" step to skip (but detrimental to the success of your organization). Leaders must set clearly defined metrics that can be discovered through data research and thoughtful discussions. Leaders can't measure progress if they don't have a benchmark for determining where they started and where they need to be.

4. *Wasted Time*

The fourth and final reason why some leaders skip the step in the Leadership Cycle is that they see it as a waste of time. Steve Jobs is widely attributed with the assertion, "It doesn't make sense to hire smart people and tell them what to do. We hire smart people so they can tell us what to do." His statement is absolutely true. However, because people are smart and driven, it doesn't mean that they can navigate through all the technical and adaptive nuances of dealing with people and their beliefs and actions.

Being smart may get people their jobs, but it doesn't always keep them there. One of the most challenging tasks on this planet is dealing with people. Effective leaders make sure everyone is heading in the right direction with all the resources in place to accomplish the mission. Hire smart people, but monitor what they do and measure their progress so that they can strive for excellence.

The right measurement establishes vital feedback loops that provide information on whether the approaches are moving the organization toward its goals. Accurate measurement helps separate the useful work from the useless work, saving everyone time in the process. Effective measures are tools that reveal whether all the training, activities, actions, planning, processes, and professional development sessions are producing results. Those tools help leaders see through the dust storms produced by so many particles of enthusiastic "busywork," which can create the illusion of progress.

Remember, just because you're moving forward, it doesn't always mean you're progressing. My friend and I found that out the hard way when we went an hour off our course to New York. If the biggest argument to skip providing measurement and feedback is time, isn't it ironic that step in the Leadership Cycle *saves* time in the long run?

Reflective Activity 9.1: "Determining Measurement Challenges"

Identify challenges that may impede your ability to effectively measure for improvement. Then, brainstorm possible solutions that will help you overcome that challenge.

Challenge	Possible Solution

Let's Talk about Feedback

We've briefly touched on feedback above, but to really understand it, we need to explore feedback further. Here is a little story:

Nicole manages a coffee shop in Seattle. As she cleans off the counter, her eyes land on a customer finishing his coffee. He reaches into his pocket, takes out his cell phone, and begins to make a call. The coffee shop is unusually quiet that day, so Nicole can't help but overhear the customer's conversation.

"Hi, I'm calling about the regional manager position you posted online a few months ago," the customer says. Intrigued, Nicole stops wiping the counter.

"Oh, I see, the position has been filled. Are you satisfied with the new manager? You are. That's great. Thank you." He hangs up the phone and carefully places it back into his pocket. He stands up, gathers his things, and approaches the counter to leave a tip in the jar for the quality service he has received.

"I couldn't help but overhear," Nicole says. "I'm sorry the job wasn't available."

The customer looks confused for a moment, and then he laughs. "What? Oh, that!" he says in a voice different than the one he used on his call (anonymity can help foster honest feedback). "That's my job, actually. I was calling to see how I was doing."

Effective leaders actively seek feedback because they understand it's the only way to course correct and improve performance. No leader is perfect, and there is always room for improvement and elevation. Quality feedback establishes a point-in-time "here" and suggestions to get to "there." Perhaps there is no better analogy for emphasizing the importance of feedback and follow-through than that of sports.

The Follow-Through

Coaches are notorious for providing feedback to the best of the best. Players welcome that feedback because they understand and value improvement. Baseball pitchers need the proper follow-through to manipulate the ball appropriately. Golfers need the proper follow-through to perfect their drives and putts. Basketball players must have the correct positioning and footing on their free throws in order to increase their percentages and optimize their form. Tennis players are constantly told by their coaches to follow through on their swings to achieve maximum accuracy and power.

Follow-through is essential for leaders too. For leaders, it is about the consistency of following up with others, and themselves, during and after the completion of a task. Giving and receiving feedback effectively is equally as important for leaders as follow-through is for athletes. Without it, leaders alienate their people and leave loose threads hanging.

Team members often will assume they are doing the right thing only to produce lackluster results. Or team members will do the right thing, but be unsure of its impact due to lack of feedback. It works both ways.

But when feedback is delivered and received regularly, engagement rises, productivity increases, and an organization becomes more closely aligned with its vision.

Effective leaders understand the importance of continual communication. It means establishing a culture where giving and receiving feedback is a regular occurrence. Gone are the days where teacher evaluations are the only time teachers receive feedback. Leaders who only rely on teacher evaluations as the vehicle for feedback delivery face many potential issues.

First, teachers may dread evaluation day because it feels like they are being "graded" themselves. Second, teachers may produce results leading up to the evaluation, but then resume their "old" way of doing things afterward. Third, teachers may not feel evaluations are important if there is a lack of follow-through and if impact hasn't been correlated to the evaluation. Therefore, feedback should be honest, timely, and continual.

Reception of Feedback

You can spot an ineffective leader a mile away when they take feedback personally and see continual communication as a threat. It is the effective leader who responds by saying, "Thank you," with no attempts to explain or defend. Effective leaders are aware that listening is a tool for clarity and understanding, but that it doesn't equal agreement either. If the feedback requires a response, effective leaders may say, "Thank you. I will take time to process that feedback and would like to continue this conversation at another time."

Unfortunately, quality feedback is often lacking in organizations because people get so caught up in *doing* work that they don't take time to *evaluate* the work that they do. Also, sometimes egos are too fragile, and so honest feedback is not given. Third, feedback can be lacking if an organization is fix minded and thus tends to be too comfortable with where it is.

If feedback is provided, it is often ambiguous and lacks timeliness. Feedback can't be cumulative in nature because drawing connections between today's results and yesterday's behavior is quite difficult.

Imagine a game of cornhole. But let's say that your target is hidden by a dense fog. Everyone is playing the game, tossing the beanbags to the hole. Now, what if you were given three bags each day? You have to throw the bags to the best of your ability. Then, the result of your daily tosses is consolidated and given to you at the end of the month. Depending on the results, you're either rewarded or punished for the accuracy of your aim, with the usual encouragement to improve. And yet, you aren't able to see where your beanbags are landing each day. You have no idea how to adjust your technique to be more successful each day because you are not getting feedback until the end of the month. That's what cumulative feedback is like—the total sum of your cornhole tosses, no matter the environmental factors at play.

The Four Pillars of Effective Feedback

Feedback is essential to learning. Feedback needs to be timely, direct, specific, and have parameters built around it to measure success and effectiveness in the future. The lack of quality feedback is one of the largest contributors to organization, team, and personal paralysis. There are four pillars of effective feedback:

1. Goal-Referenced

The first is that feedback references a goal. Effective feedback requires that a person has a goal. Then, he or she takes action to achieve the goal followed by receiving goal-related information about his or her actions. We've already established that the major goal in an educational institution is to ensure student learning. If you are not clear on the goals, or if you fail to pay attention to the goal as the ultimate priority, then feedback can easily be focused on actions that are not likely to culminate in the achievement of the goal.

Information becomes feedback when a person is trying to achieve something and the information tells them whether they are on track or need to change course.

2. Actionable

The second pillar is that effective feedback is tangible, specific, and useful. That description sounds like a bunch of mini-pillars, but ultimately it provides actionable information. Thus, "Good job!" or "You did not do that right." Giving a C+ is not feedback at all. Learners may ask themselves, "What specifically should I change next time, based on the information?" They do not know what was "good" or "wrong" about what they did.

Actionable feedback must be provided in such a way so that it is received as helpful. Many so-called feedback situations lead to frustrations because the givers are not sufficiently descriptive. They jump to an inference from data instead of simply presenting the data. For example, a supervisor may make the unfortunate but common mistake of stating that "many students were bored in class." That remark is a judgment, not an observation. It would have been far more useful and perhaps even less debatable had the supervisor said something along the lines of, "I counted ongoing inattentive behaviors in 10 of the 24 students once the lecture was underway. The behaviors included texting under desks, sleeping on the desk and talking with other students about off-topic subjects. However, after the small-group exercise began, I saw this behavior in only two students."

Effective leaders work hard to carefully observe and comment on what they observed, based on a clear statement of goals. They know that in complex performance situations, actionable feedback about what went right is just as important as feedback about what didn't work.

3. Timely

A great problem in education, however, is untimely feedback. Vital feedback on key performances often comes days, weeks, or even months after the work has been completed. Effective leaders work to ensure that students get more timely feedback and opportunities to use it while the attempt and effects are still fresh in their minds.

Few things are worse than receiving feedback for an issue that occurred months ago. When effective leaders deliver timely feedback, it tells the recipient, "I value you and your contributions to this organization; therefore, I want to address this with you right away." When feedback is put on a "to-do" list or seems retroactive, the recipient doesn't feel as valued.

4. **Ongoing**

The final pillar of effective feedback is that feedback is a continual dialogue. Adjusting performance depends on not only receiving feedback but also having opportunities to use it. The more feedback a person can receive in real-time, the better their ultimate performance will be.

If you think about it, all highly successful computer games work that way. If you play *Candy Crush, Madden, Pac-Man, or Fortnite,* you know that the key to substantial improvement is that the feedback is both timely and ongoing. When you fail, you can immediately start over—sometimes even right where you left off—to get another opportunity to receive and learn from the feedback.

You will be hard pressed to find a good reason to avoid creating a culture of communication and feedback within any organization. Feedback is a monumental tool that provides real results and creates a strong and productive organizational culture. It costs you and your organization nothing at all! You do not need to overhaul policies and procedures. You do not need to consider large restructuring initiatives. You simply need to talk to your people on a consistent, continual basis.

Feedback reinforces individual accountability. An organization—whether large or small, corporate or not for profit, complex or traditionally structured—cannot function to its fullest if individuals do not take accountability for their projects, tasks, and behaviors. Feedback is crucial when reinforcing an individual's accountability to their commitment. Feedback provides support, guidance, and direction in a way that builds confidence.

Effective feedback is what follow-through looks like in the world of leadership. So, if you're looking for methods to improve your leadership, you should focus on the way you give and receive feedback. Measure your progress and don't just monitor, or you could end up wasting precious time and resources.

Reflective Activity 9.2: "Measuring Quality and Frequency of Feedback"

Reflective Questions:

How do you provide feedback?

In what ways are you measuring the quality of your feedback?

What evidence supports the level of quality identified?

How frequently are you providing quality feedback to your staff?

_____/Week

_____/Month

_____/Year

Which of the four pillars of effective feedback would most enhance the quality of your organization?

What are your next steps for improving the quality and frequency of your feedback?

Action	Timeline for Improvement

Key Points

- To monitor is to determine the status of an activity. Monitoring typically entails critically observing an activity or process.

- Measurement is a process used to determine value.

- Effective leaders are always looking for ways to measure impact and actively seek feedback.

- Ensuring measurement and feedback is the step most often skipped in the Leadership Cycle.

- Follow-through is about the consistency of following up with others, and themselves, during and after the completion of a task.

- Effective leaders establish a culture of continual communication and feedback to meet organizational goals.

CHAPTER 10 - ADJUSTMENT AND IMPROVEMENT

"The secret of change is to focus all of your
energy, not on fighting the old, but on building the new."

— Dan Millman

In the previous chapter, I shared my story of how my friend and I were enjoying our first ever motorcycle road trip across the U.S. and my failure to measure our progress. For a good while, as I naively navigated us further south, I was trusting the process. We were moving forward, and I thought it was in the direction we needed to go. But, as we now know, it was not. Once we determined we were an hour out of our way, it was time to adjust our course to improve our progress toward our mission.

Leaders are always going to be faced with two options after ensuring measurement and feedback. The first option is to trust the process, rely on intuition, and see if the kinks smooth out over time. The second option is to make adjustments. Either decision will have an impact on the mission. It is important to note that adjustment does not always equal improvement. However, improvement does require the right adjustments. Being able to identify when to trust the process or when to make adjustments is vital to a leader's success. That reason is why ensuring adjustment and improvement is the penultimate step in the Leadership Cycle. But first, let's distinguish the difference between the two.

The Difference between Adjustment and Improvement

There is a vast difference between *improvement* and *adjustment*. When something is improved, it is made better, as evidenced by increased value or productivity. Improvement provides a tangible benefit, usually a saving of time, money, space, effort, and/or other resources. Defining adjustment is slightly more complex. Adjustment is the practical, physical, and behavioral modification required to accept and implement new practices or ideas.

Adjustment may not lead to a tangible benefit. When we talk about making adjustments, we do not mean adjusting the goal or mission—we mean adjusting the execution of a plan or process *to achieve* the mission. Adjustment and improvement work hand in hand. Effective leaders understand the dynamic relationship between the two and ensure that people are not overwhelmed by the pressures of either.

Often, leaders only focus on technical adjustments associated with measurement and feedback, and neglect the adaptive adjustments that also need to be considered.

As you may recall from chapter 4, technical challenges are problems that are easy to identify and solve with existing resources. Technical challenges in education are related to data, strategies, interventions, pacing, and activities, just to name a few. Adaptive challenges are fluid and change with circumstances. They are unpredictable, volatile, complex. They may be hard to identify, but they are easy to deny. That's because solutions to those types of challenges usually require people to learn new ways of doing things, change their attitudes, values, and norms, and adopt an experimental mindset.

Fortunately, effective leaders have an eye for adaptive adjustments. They understand that people are naturally resistant to change. Resistance could stem from fear, past negative experiences, or feelings of pressure due to a perceived lack of time to implement the needed changes. It could even be due to a perception of lack of support. Effective leaders take the time to identify what is impeding the change effort.

Knowing precisely when to make adjustments varies. The reality is that leaders must know their milestones in relation to their final destination, or end goal, and the timeline to get there. Effective leaders ensure alignment of activity and evidence of impact. Reviewing progress and reviewing measurement indicators should be a normal part of weekly team meetings, department meetings, and one-on-ones.

The right discussions lead to the right adjustments. The right adjustments lead to the right improvements.

Some organizations, notably low-performing ones, are characterized by a remarkable inability to sense that they have problems. In such organizations, people spend much of their time fighting organizational boundaries and broken processes. They are often not clear on the mission, so they don't even know if they are moving in the "right direction." They fail to detect disconnect in alignment even when presented with feedback and measurement indicators. Thus, they have little ability to anticipate and adapt to changes when it becomes necessary. That effect is commonly observed when technological changes shift rapidly.

Effective leaders are strategic in establishing a culture that is increasingly nimble and agile as a matter of ensuring success. Success is developed with an increased ability to sense, even predict, the challenges identified in measures and the challenges provided through feedback. In addition, that ability helps people take ownership in identifying solutions accordingly.

Change requires buy-in. Effective leaders make people aware of the personal benefits of the change, not just the benefit to the organization. What's in it for them? But to be clear, their concern isn't a selfish way of thinking. In fact, it is a step in the direction of ownership of the adjustment and change. When employees don't understand why changes are happening, it can be a barrier to driving ownership and commitment, even resulting in resistance or pushback. A leading factor of why so many improvement initiatives fail is employee resistance to change.

When dealing with levels of engagement for influencing improvement with a person or situation, it is advisable to follow this good rule of thumb: If the needed adjustment or improvement affects a single person, then engage at a single-person-level. However, if the adjustment or improvement affects a large group or organization, then engage at the organizational level. In other words, address the action at the level of the impact. Small impact, small involvement. Large impact, large involvement.

So, let us say that, based on quality and timely feedback, we are seeing that improvement is needed and will require some change at the organizational level. It's a very ambiguous example, but try to apply it to something within your own organization.

The first step is to involve the right people. You need to be able to ease the change and allow the adoption of technical and adaptive transformation for a positive outcome. When dealing with improvement, it is always best to introduce the improvement in chunks when possible. You shouldn't expect total transformation in a single stroke. After all, the saying goes, "How do you eat an elephant? One bite at a time."

An example of a metaphorical elephant could be something as simple as a district-wide form going from physical (hard copy) to electronic. Let's say that by a certain date, everyone in the district will be expected to fill out and submit a form electronically. Paper forms will not be accepted. That requirement sounds simple, but when you have hundreds of people filling out the same paper form for the same situation for years, it will be perceived as a huge change to switch to the new method.

The elephant can be introduced in two chunks. The first step would be the new form rollout in printed form. Everyone can get familiar with how it looks. If anyone has questions about the hard copy, they can get those questions addressed. The second step is to complete the form electronically. As you can see, one small change at a time, sorting out the issues, listening to the feedback, acknowledging the challenges, and leading people through the change before introducing the greater change all provide people the time to adapt.

Once the process is in place, it is important that leaders do not make assumptions. Measurement and getting/receiving feedback must be a continual process. Once adjustments are made, leaders then go back, continue to monitor and measure, and provide and receive feedback from anyone impacted by the change. After those steps are in place, effective leaders continue to monitor and continue to receive and provide more feedback.

However you choose to measure, the most important thing is that you *do it*. Don't let measurement fall to the wayside. Neglecting it can happen if it fails to be a priority. Understanding how close we are to where we need to be can unfortunately take a backseat due to busyness. How else can you tell if it was truly improvement or just another misaligned adjustment? How else would you know if you're going to reach your destination? If my friend had not stopped to ensure we properly measured our progress on our trip, we would have driven all the way to the southern border of the U.S. when we needed to head north. His feedback and my willingness to adjust got us where we needed to be.

When Does the Effective Leader Trust the Process?

Data based on measurement—or information based on feedback—indicating the need to adjust or improve is critical. However, being clear about the alignment of measurement and feedback to the goal is just as critical. Effective leaders understand that some measurement indicators and/or feedback is not in alignment with the mission. Although paying too much attention to the wrong type of information can derail or prolong the process of improvement, information gleaned from such measurement or feedback shouldn't necessarily be dismissed. In fact, it could be useful for reflection.

Effective leaders are always reflecting on how they can improve. But it is important to remember that misaligned measurement or feedback may not necessarily justify the need for adjustment or improvement. The reason is because measurement or feedback is useful when it *aids* you in accomplishing the mission. Some feedback is without value because it is based on bias, prejudice, guesswork, hearsay, and sometimes ignorance. Also, measurement indicators that focus on things that will not get you to the goal are superfluous. A leader must be clear about where they are going and what they are trying to accomplish.

At this point in the leadership cycle, clarity has been ensured, strategic planning and decision-making are evident, the leader and involved personnel have been empowered, and quality feedback has been provided based on the right measures. Even though transformation and improvement is a process that can come with doubt, challenges, and even resistance, it is important to trust the process. But even those who tend to trust the process have an identified line of demarcation. It is a point when they confront the brutal fact that they need to make adjustments or initiate improvement.

I have asked multiple leaders this question: "Which of the following mistakes have you most frequently made? The mistake of waiting too long to make the necessary adjustments for improvement, or the mistake of acting too quickly instead of being patient?" In response to this question, most leaders indicate that they make the mistake of waiting too long before taking decisive action.

The fact is that every leader struggles with the tension of knowing when and how to make the proper adjustments for improvement. No leader gets it right every single time. There is no algorithm to memorize, no road map to follow, no secret hack to crack that says when to stop trusting the process and make adjustments.

Effective leaders care about their people and honor the process of change, but they never lose sight of the mission. With time, effective leaders begin to improve their decision-making and judgment process about when and how to help people adjust and improve based on the right measurement and quality feedback.

Six Questions for Adjustment Reflection

Two crucial questions are: How do you know when you have crossed the line of demarcation? When is the right time to make the shift from trusting the process to adjusting and/or improving? While there is no secret formula to determine when to adjust and when to trust the process, there are several questions effective leaders can reflect upon to guide their decision. The following are six questions to be asked (in no particular order) to stimulate your thinking when you face the decision to continue trusting the process or make adjustments.

1. **Is the decision to continue doing things the same way having a negative impact on the mission?**

   It is one thing not to be making the progress you want to make. It is quite another thing to experience challenges that are damaging to the mission. If what we're doing is having a *negative* impact on the mission, that's a good indicator that it is time to make the necessary adjustments for improvement.

2. **Does the challenge with progress have to do with the will or the skill of the people who are executing the mission?**

   When we talk about will or skill, it is critical to define both. Skill is something you can teach, provide an experience for, and empower people with. It is a technical thing. Will is an adaptive approach. It is the willingness, the ability, to want to execute the mission. One challenge of progress is to ask yourself, "Am I dealing with a technical situation or an adaptive situation?"

3. **What uncontrollable factors are at play that could cause temporary or permanent challenges to the mission?**

   We can only control what we can control.

   March 2020 was when the COVID-19 pandemic was announced as a threat to the U.S. In the weeks that followed, we watched reports of lockdowns, deaths, and overwhelmed hospitals from afar as the virus wrought tragedy, initially on the world, then closer and closer to home. We knew there would be challenges, but many didn't imagine the extent that ensued. The urgent matters that arrested our minds eventually became routine. As educators, we were consumed with social-distancing protocol, who should wear masks, and how in the world we were supposed to teach and meet virtually. At the time of this writing, although those concerns are still very much a part of our world, our level of anxiety toward them has dissipated a bit. (We now have other anxieties that keep us up late at night.) Those uncontrollable factors wreaked havoc on implementation plans and improvement initiatives. But the issue was less of a "will" or "skill" matter. It was more an issue of uncontrollable factors that affected the emotions, actions, and very lives of everyone alike.

As is the case in most organizations, uncontrollable factors arise in education, and we have to take them into consideration. Sometimes, it isn't the mission that is the problem, but rather uncontrollable factors that are prohibiting accomplishment of the mission. If the latter is the case, then helping others to focus on controllable factors in uncontrollable situations can minimize frustrations and maximize productivity.

4. **What is the timeline for progress?**

   If you have six weeks to get something done, you cannot wait five weeks to see if it's effective. Or if it is not effective, you cannot wait five weeks to make the adjustment. You need to be cognizant of the timeline and the progress to meet the goal. At the bare minimum, a measure of alignment toward the mission should occur at the half-way point in the process. A healthy formula to consider is based on a three-measure approach. The first measure is to ensure clarity. The second measure is to ensure effective implementation based on clarity. The third measure is to ensure impact and alignment based on implementation.

5. **Are the measurement indicators aligned with the right indicators that will ensure the success of the mission? What are we measuring?**

In education, the most important factor to ensure quality learning is the quality of teaching. A universal example of that concept in education is when educational leaders focus on the number of classroom observations that have been conducted in a period of time. Trying to improve teaching and ensure learning by touting the number of classroom visits is not an effective indicator to measure impact. Sure, measuring the time that educational leaders spend monitoring classroom instruction is key to development and improvement, but effective leaders want to measure the impact of administrators being in those classrooms.

Instead, effective leaders don't just measure the number of classroom walkthrough observations; they measure the alignment of the lesson objective to evidence of student learning. They measure the quality of feedback provided to the teacher to determine if growth and improvement are occurring. They measure the right indicators in order to ensure the success of the mission.

When effective leaders want to support quality teaching, they engage in coaching conversations. They also reflect with the teacher and develop a coaching cycle. Putting those tactics into practice is a better method of measuring.

6. **Is the provided feedback for change based in factual evidence that will help achieve the mission?**

Remember, feedback can be steeped in several things (bias, prejudice or fear) that are unproductive. When looking at a mission, really examine the feedback for change to determine if there is factual evidence or empirical measures that will help reach the goal.

As leaders think through those questions, it's not surefire, but it's a good way to understand whether to continue to trust the process, work out the kinks because a plan is in place, or determine if it is time to adjust and improve.

It's an evolving process that takes time, effort, and practice to master. But if you've followed every step in the Leadership Cycle, you are already on your way to making exceptional progress.

Reflective Activity 10.1: "Perspective for Adjustment"

Select a mission and complete the following chart:

Mission	Reflective Question	Identify Your Perspective	Identify Your Action Steps
	Is the decision to continue doing things the same way having a negative impact on the mission?		
	Does the challenge with progress have to do with the will or skill of the people executing the mission?		
	What uncontrollable factors are at play that could cause temporary or permanent challenges to the mission?		
	What is the timeline for improvement?		
	Are the measurement indicators aligned to the right indicators that will ensure the success of the mission? What is being measured?		
	Is the provided feedback for change of good quality and based on factual evidence that will help achieve the mission?		

Key Points

- Leaders are always going to be faced with two options after ensuring measurement and feedback: The first option is to trust the process; the second option is to make adjustments.

- When something is improved, it is made better as evidenced by increased value or productivity. Improvement provides a tangible benefit and usually a saving of time, money, space, effort, and other resources.

- Adjustment is the practical, physical, and behavioral modification required to accept and implement new practices or ideas.

- Change is often met with resistance. Effective leaders take the time to identify what is impeding the change effort.

- Measurement and getting/receiving feedback have to be a continual process.

- Misaligned measurement or feedback may not necessarily justify the need for adjustment or improvement.

- Engaging in reflective questions may help you determine whether to adjust or trust the process.

CHAPTER 11 - A CULTURE OF ACCOUNTABILITY AND REWARD

"Responsibility equals accountability equals ownership. And a sense of ownership is the most powerful weapon a team or organization can have."

– Pat Summitt

It is the first day of the school year, and excitement can be felt in the air. Students chatter with their peers, filling in one another on their summer adventures. Teachers admire their freshly decorated classrooms, eager to begin another year of ensuring student learning. They stand vigilant in their doorways, greeting every student with a smile and a kind word to ease any first day jitters that students may be experiencing. Pencils are sharpened, folders are shiny, and even the desks seem to gleam with a renewed cleanliness. Each new school year presents a blank page for everyone, a fresh start.

In every single classroom, the first day of school has a ritual, a tradition of sorts, that is carried out by the teacher and the students. It happens before any book is cracked open and before any universal assessment is deployed to determine learning levels. It is on that very first day where students learn what is expected of them while they are learning in the classroom. The teacher discusses the classroom rules and regulations. The teacher explains what additional supplies the students need to be productive. The teacher outlines the curriculum or, at the very least, the consequences if assignments are not turned in on time. The teacher defines success and failure.

Students learn what happens if they misbehave, if they're late, if they don't do their homework, if they cheat, if they get into a fight with their peers, if they're sent to the office, if their name is written on the board, if they receive three strikes, and the list continues. The process is called clarifying the consequence of decisions.

By ensuring the expectations and consequences on that first day, teachers set the stage for a culture of accountability. Some teachers have students sign pledges, acknowledging they are aware of the expectations set before them. Teachers will even go as far as to send a memo home to the parents to sign, acknowledging their receipt and understanding of the student expectations.

By day two or three, students should be well versed in the expectations and consequences set for the school year. It is a road map for student success. Every teacher will have their rules posted on the wall and offer handouts of classroom expectations. They will go into detail about their classroom-management plan. In this scenario, everyone is clear about what is expected and what the consequences are for violating expectations because the onus of achievement rests on that culture of accountability.

Accountability Is a Positive Thing

Ensuring a culture of accountability and reward is the final step in the Leadership Cycle. Too often, people associate accountability with reprimand and negativity. Being held accountable, by nature, can get a bad rap, especially in a world with ineffective leaders. Ineffective leaders are those who assume that professionalism equals automatic clarity of expectations. It is the *you know what's expected of you because you're a working professional* attitude that can cripple an organization, because the moment someone doesn't know what is expected of him or her, the moment they are held accountable to any degree, is the moment they feel targeted and unfairly reprimanded.

A lack of establishing a culture of consistent, clear communication frustrates so many schools and organizations. In these organizations, there is a very vivid disconnect between the mission, the vision, the lived values, and the consistency of accountability. Some people are held accountable; others are not. Perceived favoritism ensues as trust and respect are damaged. The employees held accountable take little to no ownership of their actions, instead opting to pull the "victim card" and blame anything and anyone else.

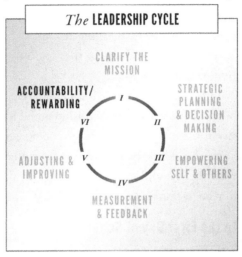

That victim card is a dangerous card to play. When an employee is in the victim mindset, they feel nothing but fear, panic, and anxiety. The second they are held accountable for their actions, that person automatically assumes termination is on the table. They mistrust their leader because now they fear the leader is "out to get them." Those feelings and perceptions can drive an employee to contact their local union representative, vent their feelings of unfair treatment to their colleagues, and rally to find supporters who sympathize with their plight. But that reaction can be avoided or at least minimized. Accountability is not a negative thing, nor does it ever have to be met with fear, anxiety, and mistrust.

Here are three very important questions about accountability for every leader:

1. Do your employees know the measures being used to hold them accountable?

2. Are your employees clear about the impact of accountability on them personally and professionally?

3. Do your employees understand what accountability looks like, sounds like, and even feels like?

Somewhere along the way, consequences have come to be viewed as unfavorable. The ironic truth is that consequences can be either positive or negative. The origin of the word consequence comes from two Latin words: *con*, meaning "together," and *sequi*, meaning "to follow." Combined, they make a neutral word meaning "something that logically or naturally follows from an action or condition."

Often, the discomfort of consequence is rooted in the misbelief that the hidden agenda of consequence means "punishment." However, the word can also mean "rewards." In my experience, the people who don't like consequences are those who consistently underperform in their jobs. High performers, on the other hand, love consequences. To them, the word is synonymous with recognition and reward.

Let's Go Back to the First Day of School

Imagine what would have happened if a principal took the same approach at the beginning of the school year with his or her staff. Everyone is gathered together as the principal communicates, not simply to be heard, but to be understood. The teachers' expectations are clearly written and articulated in the meeting. Teachers are informed about the consequences of their own actions in a comprehensive and supportive manner. Principals go as far as to discuss what actions warrant each consequence.

For example, the principal may create a hypothetical scenario to articulate what decisions may warrant a memorandum of concern, a written reprimand, peer coaching, and even termination from employment. Then, take it a step further and explain the impact each corrective or coaching action will have on an individual's career, personnel file, evaluation, or contract. Its purpose isn't to instill fear within the teachers, but rather to lay out the expectations in a clear and concise manner so that teachers can perform their duties with knowledge and within a culture of accountability.

Imagine a principal who engages in discussion, answers questions, and listens to concerns. The principal establishes transparent practices in alignment with the mission, vision, and values of the campus. The principal takes the time to get feedback from staff about ways to improve the process and incorporate ideas, suggestions, and input that is reasonable, feasible, and adds value to the process. The approach will not stop employees from violating rules and expectations, but it does eliminate the anxiety, fear, and uncertainty that often comes with accountability.

Clarity improves a team's ability to execute plans. It enhances a team's ability to change directions confidently and elevates a sense of ownership. When clarity is abundant in terms of consequence, the feeling of being targeted or singled out is drastically minimized. When clarity of expectations is delivered in a supportive and caring manner, individuals realize that a culture of accountability is a positive force for the individual, the students, and the organization at large.

When Ownership Is Dormant

Nothing is as destructive as irresponsibility, which I define as not being answerable to authority. It means lacking a sense of accountability. It also means, fickle, careless, thoughtless, undependable, and unstable. To be irresponsible is to transfer blame for your behavior to someone else.

Ineffective leaders allow people not to take responsibility for their actions, decisions, situations, or circumstances. People with a propensity to disavow ownership are experts at blaming the past for their future. A byproduct of their attitude is a culture of irresponsibility where everyone engages in the blame game. The principal blames the teachers for test scores. The teachers blame administration for student behavior. The assistant principals blame the teachers for student behavior. The upperclassmen teachers blame the lowerclassmen teachers for unprepared students with learning deficiencies. The parents blame the teachers for their children not passing a test, or even the entire grade. The teachers blame the parents for their children not engaging in the classroom activities and their own education. The principal blames the central office for the campus situation. In turn, the central office blames the campus for their situation.

The blame goes back and forth, around and around, and improvement doesn't happen, trust breaks down, and no one wins.

Establishing a Culture of Accountability

Establishing a culture of accountability is paramount for the success of the organization, and encompasses the students, teachers, faculty, staff, and administration. I often ask educational leaders two questions. The first is, "What is your definition of accountability?" I follow this question with, "How do you establish a culture of accountability?"

Here's what I learned. The leader says something along the lines of, "Holding someone accountable means following up with them, discussing more about the situation at hand, or reminding them of the expectation." Sometimes, the leader is dogmatic in their approach and thinks accountability is beating people over the head with memoranda of concern and threatening corrective action based on every mistake. Neither of those approaches will be successful in transforming an organization from a mindset of apathy and lack of ownership to one of passion and buy-in.

You see, the first answer sounds good. It is a very common definition of accountability. It might actually be where accountability got such a bad rap. But "reminding them of the expectation" and "following up with them" are passive approaches. Sure, the leader is "active" in the delivery of communication, but the recipients, those who failed to meet expectations, are passive. They are reminded. They are asked to listen. Where is the action in that approach? Where is the transference of ownership from the leader to the colleague?

In a nutshell, accountability is giving a reckoning for one's conduct and reporting on one's progress. It is also an admission of motives and reasons for taking certain actions. When building a culture of accountability, effective leaders understand their role in the process. They understand most people have not been trained to solve problems but rather, to bring problems to a person higher up in the organization to solve. That mindset is a challenge. It takes time for leaders to establish a culture where problems are reasonably and effectively solved at the lowest level.

There are two questions effective leaders can ask that have a powerful impact on the accountability process. When dutifully presented with a problem, effective leaders can ask, "How are you planning to overcome this challenge?" That response may take employees aback, for they have been used to presenting problems to their leaders and walking away from them. Therefore, the second question is equally important. "What support is needed to assist you?" Accountability does not mean the leader shoulders the weight for every single problem in the organization. It also doesn't mean the employees must navigate problems and issues alone without counsel.

By asking those questions time and time again, effective leaders create the understanding that they are not there to solve every problem, but can provide the resources, support, coaching, and training to help others be successful. Conversely, ineffective leaders cannot fight off the urge to solve other people's problems, which is what limits their ability to be highly successful. Each time someone comes to an ineffective leader with a problem and the leader solves it, a loop of dependency is strengthened. That act in turn develops a culture of reliance instead of a culture of ownership. It fosters a mindset of compliance instead of comprehension. Additionally, it perpetuates a reactive disposition instead of a proactive belief system.

The culture of dependency is rarely built from an egotistical place. In most cases, the ineffective leader is not intentionally forcing his or her employees to depend on them. The pattern comes from a willingness to be there for everyone and create positive progress. However, solving everyone's problems will not encourage accountability.

There are three major inhibitors to accountability:

1. *Planning in place of action.* In education, we are so good at planning. We have lesson plans, classroom-management plans, five-year plans, district-wide plans, statewide plans—the list goes on. We can plan our hearts out. But when action does not take place in the midst of all our planning, it is impossible to establish a culture of account-

ability. Effective leaders ensure the elimination of the gap between planning and action.

2. *Excuses instead of execution.* There will always be barriers to knock down when executing plans in any system. However, developing excuses as the reason that barriers are "impenetrable" will quickly destroy any semblance of a culture of accountability. Remember, accountability isn't about excuses. It is about empowerment, ownership, and action. An established culture of excuses will lead to inconsistency in accountability. Effective leaders are very skilled at redirecting any attempt to justify or provide excuses as well as at leading people through the thinking process to take ownership of their situation. Such leaders focus their time, energy, effort, resources, and dialogue on impacting what they can control.

3. *Focus on being busy rather than on impact.* "I'm so busy." "I'm so overwhelmed." "I don't have time for anything else." If you hear those phrases often, you know you have a culture where busyness is shown as a badge of honor. But it is not. Busyness is an excuse for not achieving results. Busy is hurried. Busy is overwhelmed. Busy is fast and careless. Busy is a series of sprints around the track, ignoring exchange zones and gripping that baton with the selfish ambition of finishing the team race all by yourself. Certainly, there are moments when life gets busy. We all get that. But when busy extends to being tired, worn out, and exhausted without evidence of impact, it is not productive. We never want to look back at life and say, "Wow, I was really good at being busy."

When you hear language such as, "What is my impact?" and "What evidence do I have that I am being effective and efficient?" you know you have a culture where results are far more important than any level of activity.

Growing a Culture of Accountability

The beauty of accountability is that the leader only needs to start the ball rolling. The effective leader plants seeds of accountability, steps back, and watches the team water those seeds. Once accountability takes hold in the organization, more and more people will come to your aid. Teams hold one another accountable, even in the leader's absence. It all starts with creating a psychologically safe environment where people challenge one another in a supportive manner and look into collaborating for success. Is accountability working that way in your school? Why or why not?

Conventional wisdom holds that lack of accountability is a worker problem. Ineffective leaders lament that the declining work ethic and rampant apathy within an organization is due to the job. A lack of loyalty is a "worker issue." Employees rent their jobs instead of owning them. That way of thinking encourages the ineffective leader to blame employees, makes accountability personal, and defaults to punitive consequences.

What if conventional wisdom is wrong? What if the lack of accountability is purely a leadership problem? It all adds up. When you have leaders who inspire ownership and employees who trade time for money, you may be surprised that the difference has less to do with strategies and techniques and everything to do with the leaders' mindset.

The best leaders are guided by the following beliefs:

1. ***Employees want to do a good job and succeed.*** Yes, it is a job, but most people are driven by personal success and grow from witnessing their impact in any organization.

2. ***Consequences should be taught and sustained rather than used to mandate compliance.*** Consequences used to mandate compliance can feel very demotivating. That methodology generates a huge feeling of mistrust throughout the organization, as well as a culture of fear.

3. ***Relationships, not position, are the ultimate tool for influencing the performance of others.*** The difference between mandated compliance and volunteered commitment can be traced to the relationship between the leader and follower. People will do what they are told to do because it is their job. They will run through walls to succeed for a leader they trust and admire. Employees show up

on their first day at work wanting to take ownership and succeed. Somewhere along the way, some will decide to do as little as possible. How many employees take that path may very well depend on you.

Those leaders who get accountability right know that most people want to do great work. They view their job as creating an environment where commitment and self-discipline are volunteered. Effective leaders are clear about what they expect from themselves, their organization, and those who work for them. They walk the walk. They communicate those expectations. Remember, people can't hear you think. You really don't want to make people guess what you want them to do. Unspoken expectations lead to resentment. Here are three things you can do right now to build a culture of volunteered accountability:

1. *Adjust your mindset.* There may be a few people on your team who do not want to do a good job, but that number is very small—probably 2%–5%. Stop thinking of the other 95%–98% as part of the problem.

2. *Make sure you are doing your part.* Be honest with yourself on areas where you are not fulfilling your responsibility and make a plan to improve. Solicit feedback if you're unsure of blind spots. Determine in which areas you are lacking processes and systems to "ensure" impact.

3. *Focus relentlessly on relationships.* People will always be your greatest asset. Your ability to connect with, inspire, and motivate them matters. The organizational structure is rooted in relationships, not titles. When employees feel psychologically safe, valued, and understand their impact, relationships are strong throughout the organization. Accountability is not a thing to be feared but rather, a culture to be embraced.

In his book, *Good Authority,* Jonathan Raymond says, "The right question isn't, 'How do I get my people to engage?' The right question is, 'How do I engage better with my people?'"

Reward and Recognition

Reward and recognition are so powerful that these two elements can bring about a renewed sense of employee loyalty, ownership in the mission, and pride. Recognition connects employees to the organization, elevates performance, and increases retention.

From an early age, we crave recognition from our parents, our teachers, and our friends. It never truly goes away. Simple acts of acknowledgement remain a major boost for employee morale and performance. When we are developing and receive a positive affirmation, we begin to trust the feedback we receive. We know the giver of feedback is not out to get us. He or she is working to help us develop. As a result, we can receive constructive feedback with a neutral reaction, knowing the person giving feedback has a positive intent in supporting our growth, instead of perceiving it as a negative affirmation toward us.

Employee recognition helps to retain top talent, increase employee engagement, and encourage high performance. All three of those factors help everyone strive to make a positive and measurable impact to the overall mission and vision of the organization.

My challenge to leaders is this: Channel that first day of school excitement with your staff. Pair it with a clear and transparent conversation about expectations, what-if scenarios, and the personal, professional, and organizational impact that specific choices and behaviors will have on the entire mission as a whole. When everyone knows what is expected and are given the tools, resources, and support to course correct when necessary, a culture of accountability will continue to grow. A culture of accountability will be welcomed.

The Differences between a Culture of Accountability and a Culture of Nonaccountability

To ensure clarity, let's explore a culture of accountability and a culture of nonaccountability in a simple chart as follows:

	Culture of Nonaccountability	Culture of Accountability
Belief	People are the problem	People are the solution
	Challenges divide	Challenges unite
	Fixed mindset	Growth mindset
	Blame	Ownership
Focus	The person	The issue
	The past	The future
	Punishment and embarrassment	Correction and restoration
	Fault finding	Fact-finding
	Compliance to do the job	Learning to do the job better
Results	Assuming	Ensuring
	Informing	Empowering
	Low levels of trust	Higher levels of trust
	Reactive behavior	Proactive behavior
	Confusion	Clarity
	Status quo	Risk-takers
	Unclear priorities	Clear priorities
	Stagnation or regression	Constant growth
	Lower levels of team morale	Higher levels of team morale
	Higher degrees of turnover	Lower degrees of turnover
	Less employee engagement	More employee engagement

Reflective Activity 11.1: "Culture of Accountability"

Read each of the following questions and select the number that best correlates to your current organizational culture of accountability:

To what degree do people at all levels take ownership for solving problems, with a focus on continuous improvement instead of playing the victim and blaming others?

Low   1   2   3   4   5   6   7   8   9   10 High

To what degree is the culture directly linked to student achievement and measured?

Low   1   2   3   4   5   6   7   8   9   10 High

To what degree are people regularly acknowledged and recognized for their value and contribution as opposed to relying on formal/structured recognitions or awards?

Low   1   2   3   4   5   6   7   8   9   10 High

To what degree is busyness valued more than productivity/impact?

Low   1   2   3   4   5   6   7   8   9   10 High

To what degree are poor performers addressed, coached, supported, or removed instead of ignored, transferred, or promoted?

Low   1   2   3   4   5   6   7   8   9   10 High

To what degree do people openly surface and effectively resolve problems and conflicts rather than avoiding them?

Low   1   2   3   4   5   6   7   8   9   10 High

To what degree do people at all levels have a clear sense of direction, purpose, and priorities rather than dealing with fragmented, competing, or overwhelming priorities?

Low   1   2   3   4   5   6   7   8   9   10 High

To what degree are student outcomes, teacher team execution, and campus outcomes tracked and measured instead of only generic metrics?

Low   1   2   3   4   5   6   7   8   9   10 High

To what degree do administrators effectively collaborate, problem solve, and include others in the decision-making processes rather than operate in isolation?

Low   1   2   3   4   5   6   7   8   9   10 High

To what degree do people initiate and execute change rather than resisting or avoiding change?

Low   1   2   3   4   5   6   7   8   9   10 High

Score	Results
0–60	Your score indicates – A critically low level of accountability. This means a very high probability of inefficient practices, and/or low levels of morale within the organization.
61–79	Your score indicates – A low level of accountability. This means that your organization is experiencing breakdowns in execution that may negatively affect student achievement, compounded by wasted resources, employee frustration, and low levels of efficiency.
80–89	Your score indicates – A moderate level of accountability. This means that your organization is fairly accountable. In order to be even more influential to ensure student achievement, the organization must improve its execution of good practices as well as cross-functional teamwork and engagement.
90–100	Your score indicates – An excellent level of accountability. Congratulations! Your organization is a great place to work where all stakeholders are treated well and the organization exhibits a high level of execution and cross-functional teamwork.

Key Points

- Ensuring a culture of accountability and reward is the final step in the Leadership Cycle.

- In an organization where the culture of accountability is muddy, employees held accountable take little to no ownership of their actions, instead opting to pull the "victim card" and blame anything and anyone else.

- When clarity is delivered in a supportive and caring manner, individuals realize that a culture of accountability is a positive force for the individual, the students, and the organization at large.

- Nothing is as destructive as irresponsibility.

- People with a propensity to not take ownership are experts at blaming the past for their future.

- When building a culture of accountability, effective leaders understand that most people have not been trained to solve problems; rather, they have been trained to bring problems to a person higher up in the organization to solve.

- There are three major inhibitors to accountability: planning in place of action, offering excuses in place of execution, and focusing on being busy rather than on impact.

- Reward and recognition are so powerful that these two elements can bring about a renewed sense of employee loyalty, ownership in the mission, and pride. Recognition connects employees to the organization, elevates performance, and increases retention.

CHAPTER 12 - PRECISE HIRING

"People are not your most important asset. The right people are."

– Jim Collins

Congratulations! You have made it all the way through the Leadership Cycle.

I hope you have gleaned important lessons and knowledge that will help you transform your educational leadership landscape. Remember, everything you need to make monumental changes is already within you. Just follow the steps of the Leadership Cycle and you will see results.

But before we conclude the collection of lessons, there is one more important topic I want to address. It is not a step in the Leadership Cycle, but is undoubtedly related to everything you are trying to achieve as a leader—especially when it comes to fulfilling the mission and vision.

The two most important decisions regarding staff that a leader will make are whom they hire and whom they fire. If the first is not done well, the second will be done frequently. There are a plethora of methods for hiring that can positively affect the likelihood of success. The following information is by no means prescriptive. However, it contains proven strategies you can deploy that align with best practices for hiring with the result of a greater probability of success.

Effective principals hire quality teachers. They are able to use the interview process to identify characteristics of quality teachers that will respond positively to leadership. It should come as no surprise that principals directly affect their students' levels of achievement. Principals are in a unique position to use the hiring process to increase student achievement. For example, Branch, et al. (2012) examined value-added scores and found that just one year of having a highly effective principal who hires the right teachers and provides proper support increased student achievement from the 50th percentile to more than the 54th percentile.

When you hire high-quality teachers who respond well to leadership, you are cultivating a culture of trust and accountability, which translates to an environment in which alignment with the mission is more prevalent. More than any reform strategy or campus-wide policy, effective teaching that ensures learning is the best way to improve student achievement.

The same is true in the reverse. Hiring teachers who are more focused on teaching than on student learning can lead not only to a lack of student achievement, but will also create much more work for everyone around them. Students will notice a teacher who is unwilling to respond appropriately to leadership direction or who is not intrinsically motivated to learn, grow, and develop in alignment with the mission and vision of the organization, staff members, and parents. Once that deviation occurs, the mission is in jeopardy, and the culture is compromised.

Ultimately, it is the principal's job to ensure a healthy culture and climate. Have you heard the adage, "Culture eats strategy for breakfast?" And that declaration is true regardless of the strategies employed to ensure learning. Culture sets the standard for building a high-performance environment.

The Difference between Culture and Climate

We have talked about *organizational culture* and *climate* many times throughout this book. Those terms are often used interchangeably, but they are not synonymous. When we are defining climate in an education setting, the term refers to the characteristics that differentiate one school from another and includes the feeling that stakeholders have when they are in the school. School climate represents the attitude of the organization.

In a healthy climate, teachers are happy. The collective mood is positive and focused on student achievement. Leaders must create conditions where positivity, proactiveness, and happiness thrive. Unfortunately, some leaders do not research the most effective strategies for creating a healthy climate, instead relying on extrinsic rewards. Bringing muffins to the teachers each week may give a few teachers that extra needed boost, but the act will not affect the morale of the building. Activities designed to address low morale by creating a more positive climate need to be scrutinized using the following criteria:

- How much of an investment in time and energy is involved?

- What is the span of time it takes for the activity to have an impact?

- Will the activity impact an individual or the group?

- Is the activity focused on intrinsic or extrinsic rewards?

- How does this activity align with the culture?

Activities that go deeper include open and honest town halls with the staff, team-building activities, brainstorming sessions where actionable items are deployed within timeframes (and not just strategized and talked about), to name just a few examples.

Descriptions of culture go deeper than that of climate. Culture includes the history of the school (or any organization), including the traditions and rituals that develop over time. Culture is developed from or composed of three levels: (1) artifacts, (2) values, and (3) basic assumptions.

Artifacts are aspects of the school that are observable. They include the physical layout of the building, the dress code, the feel of the building, and even the smell of the building. *Values* are the ideologies and philosophies that guide how things should be done. Lastly, *basic assumptions* are the process and feelings that guide the behavior and action of individuals within the school. For example, when provided with feedback for improvement, is the prevailing assumption one of self-reflection, positive intent, and a continuous improvement mindset? Or is it one of deflection, blame, criticism, and a lack of ownership?

When we're talking about culture, we're talking about mindset, behavior, and experience. In a healthy, student-focused culture, people respond appropriately to stressful or challenging situations and keep the focus on learning instead of teaching. By their response, people create the culture's energy by working collaboratively in teams, departments, pods, and small groups. People are the life force of the organization, so it is vital that you hire contributors, not detractors.

The impact of hiring high-quality teachers spans even further past establishing a culture and climate that ensures student achievement. The results of hiring effective educators affect the school budget. School administrators witness thousands of dollars in savings accrue when they do not have to spend scarce resources to retrain, reorient, micromanage, support, counsel, or release ineffective teachers. Every time an administrator has to replace a poor hire, it costs the organization money. The hiring process, training, onboarding, and orientation for new hires is not cheap. Beyond finances, it takes up valuable time, resources, effort, energy, and focus. Based on those factors alone, it is crucial to hire the best teachers the first time around.

You will be hard pressed to find a principal who does not eventually admit that he or she has made at least one hiring mistake in their career. Many try to correct those mistakes by investing a great deal of resources, time, and effort into supporting improvement and attempting to change the mindset of the bad hire. Then, there are others who default to releasing hires who do not meet expectations.

So, how can school leaders ensure they effectively identify quality teachers before they indulge in restorative practices aimed at salvaging their poor hiring decisions? It all starts with the interview.

Examining the Interview Process

Throughout the years in education, the hiring process has been criticized as both bureaucratic and ineffective. After all, if the goal of hiring the best is to ensure student achievement, why are there so many students who do not achieve when the best have been hired? The demand for teachers remains remarkably high, so the process is often rushed and ill advised. The hiring window is often short and sandwiched between the end of the school year and beginning of a new school year. A compressed timeline presents many challenges, but it should also inspire administrators to develop highly impactful interview processes and procedures that truly explore the talents, determination, skill sets, and passion of each candidate.

Traditionally, the interview process is meant to provide insight into a candidate's future performance by asking questions and obtaining oral responses. Yet, researchers have studied many facets of the interview process and produced mixed results related to the predictive validity of the employment interview (2007).

People tend to present their best self at the interview, and that presentation may not always correlate to day-to-day job performance. Despite that factor, a carefully designed interview process can still provide administrators a unique opportunity to determine how people accomplish results, not just what they have accomplished in the past.

Obviously, administrators can only ensure their students receive a first-rate education if a strategy for recruiting, hiring, and retaining high-quality teachers is followed. It may be time to reevaluate the interview process.

Teacher selection deserves rigorous examination to ensure the alignment between the candidate and the school's core values and pedagogical practices to identify teachers with the greatest likelihood of increasing student outcomes. Michael Fullan (2008) argued that effective hiring consists of more than just matching candidates to profiles, but of finding those who fit in the organizational culture. Successful candidates are more than just their GPA and certifications; they are individuals who understand the nuances of building relationships, the importance of impact, and the value of a growth mindset, and yearn to add value to the environment.

Emotional Intelligence and the Interview Process

It is a fair assumption that the higher a person's IQ, the higher their intelligence. However, today's psychologists assign more factors to determine an individual's intelligence. Now, emotional intelligence (EQ), including the social, personal, and survival components of an individual, is considered equally important, particularly for work performance. In fact, the foundational competency of great performance is considered to be based on EQ.

Lynn (2008) stated that 70% of abilities essential for effective performance are related to emotional competencies and not personality. Emotional intelligence includes one's ability to understand both themselves and others, their ability to relate to others, and their ability to adapt and cope with their immediate surroundings, which determine one's ability to successfully deal with environmental demands.

When an individual has high emotional intelligence, they are able to manage critical situations in both their personal and professional lives. How beneficial would it be for hiring managers to assess a candidate's emotional intelligence as part of the interview process?

Ghanizadeh and Moafian (2020) conducted a study designed to explore how a teacher's emotional intelligence influenced their pedagogical success. The results? A high correlation between the two. After all, teaching involves managing critical situations. It involves interpersonal relationships and the ability to motivate and inspire others. Teachers constantly have to "read the room" to determine the best way to ensure learning. Let's not forget the many emotional situations that occur inside and outside of the classroom, with parents and students alike.

One of the most effective ways to make accurate predictions about a candidate's EQ is to engage in behavior-based interviewing to identify past behaviors, activities, and results. Properly assessing EQ can provide information that is critical to organizations and can greatly improve the hiring process. Behavior-based interviewing allows everyone on the hiring side to assess whether candidates are reflective, if they tend to act with intention, or if they react to certain stressors. In addition, interviewers can assess whether the applicant takes ownership of their responsibilities, tends to blame others, or displays an offensive arrogance or defensiveness. The candidate's reflections provide a wealth of information about their personality and behaviors, which can help distinguish the benefits and risks associated with hiring them.

You may be wondering how one can determine a candidate's EQ. What questions does one ask? What scenarios can one play out? Interviewers can use behavior-based interview (BBI) questions to explore whether candidates have exhibited job-related behavior in previous work-related situations. The basic premise of the behavioral interview is the underlying assumption that past performance is a good predictor of future performance.

For example, in an educational setting, the building principal may inquire about a time when the applicant went above and beyond to ensure student learning, what motivated their actions, and what the outcome was. Sometimes the best way to determine a candidate's EQ is to give them an exercise to complete prior to the interview.

Shaking Up the Interview Process

At the beginning of this book, I shared with you my experience as a first-time principal. I didn't get everything right the first time around. I came into the role wanting to change everything and did not quite follow the Leadership Cycle in order. In time, I understood the impact I could make on the school. I developed ways to ensure learning and clarity in the mission.

Later in my career, as a high school principal, we were awarded recognition as one of America's Best Urban Schools by the National Center for Urban School Transformation. In the span of four years, we earned 22 distinctions.

A single distinction in Texas is hard to come by, let alone 22. We didn't close achievement gaps at a staggering rate simply based on how intelligent the teachers were, how good the faculty believed they were, or even how hard everyone worked. We accomplished amazing feats as a team due to our ability to respond appropriately to the adversities and challenges that came with ensuring teaching and learning. We were intentional about our culture, climate, systems, beliefs, and whom we invited to align themselves to the work of our mission and vision. The rationale was that there is nothing that affects learning more than the teacher you put in front of the students.

As principal, I developed a team that invested a lot of our time in interviewing and scrutinizing the hiring process, making sure we developed an effective process that got us the right people in the right seats. Sometimes that meant we were interviewing 20 to 30 people for one position. There were times, due to untimely resignations or other issues out of our control, when we had to hire only the candidates who were available. Still, we had to make quality hiring decisions based on a quality hiring process.

And if we wanted to gauge EQ proactively, we needed to find a way to have candidates demonstrate their EQ. One way we accomplished it was to provide interviewees a data set prior to our interview meeting with clear directives to bring the data with them to the interview. At the time of the interview, if they had not interacted with the data, analyzed it, or even remembered it, that shortfall gave us great insight into their level of preparedness, proactiveness, level of communication, etc.

On the other hand, we would have interviewees call us before the interview to inquire about the data, looking for clarity to ensure understanding. And that was all we were looking for. The team wanted to see the mindset of how they approached the data. Some people sat down, analyzed the data, looked things up, and took notes. We were not interested in the data per se, but in how they approached the data, how they communicated when they were not clear, how they prioritized the provided directions, and how they took ownership of their decisions. Those behaviors would tell us how they would approach the job at hand.

Another example we used was a lesson demonstration. We provided interviewees a lesson plan in advance and asked them to prepare a 10-minute lesson for the committee. Now, that request is not an abnormal practice. Plenty of schools have interviewees teach a lesson, some even in front of students. However, the focus here was a bit more intentional. Our hiring team purposely gave them way too much material, making it impossible to cover in the short timeframe. Some interviewees would come in and try to teach the whole thing, doing a great job of trying to finish their prepared lesson in the time allotted. Most of these interviewees never checked for clarity or understanding.

Later, during the discussion portion of the interview, we would ask the candidate the following question: "Is it more important to you that you cover all intended material on pace with the scope and sequence, or that you ensure student learning prior to moving forward with lessons?" We would then sit and listen to 99% of the interviewees pontificate about how they believed whole heartedly in ensuring student learning prior to moving forward with the lesson.

I would then interject with the question, "Then why did you fly through the lesson we provided for you?" Their response would always be, "Well, I only had 10 minutes and wanted to get through as much as possible." See, we were not trying to trip them up, but by just asking the question, they would not have told us anything of value. By having a way to correlate their behavior to their response, we were able to glean much more about how they think.

On the flip side, we also saw candidates who stopped after the 10 minutes, only making it through a fraction of the lesson. These interviewees would make statements such as, "I do not want to move forward until I'm sure you are comfortable with what we just covered." That answer was the golden ticket. It was the teaching approach we wanted to see in each and every one of our classrooms.

Those are just a few of the interview exercises that allowed us to see how the candidates thought and processed information. However, during my experience as a principal, I've learned how to identify clear red flags in the process that I would like to share with you.

Interview Red Flags

For the person or group responsible for selecting the right candidate for the job, the interviewing radar must go far beyond detecting basic qualities of a candidate. Many signs such as nervousness, thoughtful pauses, or a slightly tense demeanor can safely be ignored during the interview process, but here are nine red flags that should never be ignored:

1. **The candidate shows up late or not at all.** There are always extenuating circumstances that can be overlooked. These are situations that are beyond one's control such as hospitalization, family emergencies, and unforeseen transportation issues. However, those instances are rare and usually warrant a courtesy call for being late. When there is

no call and no show, you have a clear sign of disregard and disrespect for the opportunity and the interviewer's time.

2. **The qualifications on their resume don't match up with their responses.** When you ask about specific qualifications and the candidate has a difficult time answering your questions, there is a chance he or she falsified stated qualifications. Needless to say, a person who falsifies their qualifications is more likely to be dishonest in their work. Trust and dependability are everything, so do not let this red flag fly.

3. **There is a disconnect between their activity and evidence of their impact.** You have a candidate who can rattle off the list of the multiple committees they have served on, the list of plans they have developed, or the litany of professional developments they have facilitated or attended. The problem is these admissions are just "busy lists" when the candidate fails to articulate any evidence of the impact on student achievement. That red flag indicates the candidate may be more focused on activity than on result.

4. **Their enthusiasm is anything but present.** There are some incredibly good reasons why someone avoids showing enthusiasm. Perhaps they don't want to appear too eager or they have trouble regulating emotions. But, in most cases, if a candidate doesn't interact positively with a firm handshake, eye contact, and a smile, they're not truly enthused about the job. Often, a disengaged interviewee makes for a disengaged employee.

5. **The candidate is disrespectful, arrogant, or overly self-assured.** The humble-brag is difficult to master, and a candidate always walks a fine line between being confident and being arrogant. Notice how the candidate interacts with everyone in the building. If they talk down to the janitorial staff or front office, that is a red flag. If they are inconsiderate of space in the waiting room, or are busy texting instead of making a good impression, that is a red flag. In

the interview, a red flag should pop up when a candidate tries to control the conversation by interrupting and consistently steering the conversation back to them.

6. **The candidate speaks badly about their previous employer.** Speaking poorly of a previous employer can imply a lack of responsibility for one's actions and the inability to deal with difficult situations. That revelation is especially concerning if the candidate plays the "victim card." Additionally, a complainer can bring down the morale of an entire department, so any bad-mouthing at all is a red flag that the candidate is not worth investing in.

7. **The candidate demonstrates no evidence that they researched your organization.** A candidate who goes into an interview not knowing about the entity shows a lack of preparation as well as little genuine interest about the institution and how their prospective role would fit within the organization's goals and values. Each school is different. Each origin story and organizational makeup is different. A solid candidate will take time to explore the things that make your school stand out from others and ask thoughtful questions about their findings.

8. **The candidate doesn't take responsibility for failed projects, teams gone awry, or mistakes.** Another red flag shows up in a candidate who doesn't admit to any responsibility for past mistakes and instead blames others such as coworkers, bosses, a lack of resources, or a lack of skilled team members. When you ask, "Tell me of a time you faced a difficult project or challenging work situation," listen to what the candidate has to say. You can tell right away if they blame others for the challenges or if they take responsibility for their actions based on what anecdote they choose to share.

If the candidate was released by a former employer, it's important to listen carefully to their rationale. If they indicate they are blameless and cannot admit to errors, you likely do not want to hire that individual. The right candidate will reflect on mistakes, identify possible areas of improvement, and articulate steps taken to ensure success in the future.

9. **The candidate's most recent supervisor is not listed as a reference.** Current or previous employers have the most in-depth knowledge about an interviewee's work ethic. Leaving the most recent supervisor off the reference list can give the impression of a hidden reason that the interviewee did not want their future employer to contact their past employer.

A primary goal of the reference check is to get a third-person assessment of the candidate's achievements. One of the best ways is by using open-ended, behavioral interviewing questions like those used to interview the candidate. Set a positive tone from the outset, and let the reference speak freely and without interruption. Avoid leading questions, negative language, or anything that will put the reference on the defensive. Avoid asking broad questions such as "What can you tell me about John?" Ideally, you would refer to specifics gleaned from the candidate during the interview process. A few examples would be, "I understand John helped implement a new tracking system. Can you tell me more about his role in that?" Or "I understand there was tension in the department. Can you give me an example of how John galvanized his coworkers to work as a team?"

Follow up these behavioral assessments with general questions about communication, management, organizational, and especially people skills. Ideally, your questions will elicit detailed, specific examples without a lot of thought on the part of the reference.

Ensuring the Right People Fill the Right Seats

When you have a one-on-one interview with a candidate, there is always the possibility that interviewing bias could affect the hiring decision. That potential is natural because we all carry a bit of bias with us wherever we go.

One method for eliminating interviewing bias is establishing an interviewing team of three to five individuals with experience in the job. A group setting provides a platform for new hires to address future team members and lets current employees feel important and part of the hiring process. After all, the new hires will be interfacing with your current employees.

Remember, the key to meet educational demand is to hire individuals who are highly qualified and a good fit. High-performing institutions that use behavioral-based interviewing greatly increase their probability of successfully inviting someone onto the team who will add value in the intended areas. Such new team members often improve morale and student achievement. It is paramount to get it right the first time as much as possible. Your students, current teachers, and faculty depend on it.

Key Points

- The two most important decisions that a leader will make is whom they hire and whom they fire. If the first is not done well, the second will be done frequently.

- When you hire high-quality teachers who respond well to leadership, you are cultivating a culture of trust and accountability.

- One of the most effective ways to make accurate predictions about a candidate's emotional intelligence is to engage in behavior-based interviewing to identify past behaviors.

- When employees have high emotional intelligence, they can manage critical situations in both their personal and professional lives.

- One method for eliminating interviewing bias is establishing an interviewing team of three to five individuals with experience in the particular job.

- Climate refers to the characteristics that differentiate one school from another and includes the atmosphere felt by stakeholders when they are in the school.

- Culture includes the history of the school or history of any organization, such as the traditions and rituals that develop over time.

CONCLUSION

In 2018, Apple released a commercial for its Apple Watch, a device whose primary purpose is to monitor your health in order to help you achieve your fitness goals. The commercial begins with a man—who is not wearing an Apple Watch—sitting comfortably on his couch drinking coffee. He looks over to see a clone of himself wearing an Apple Watch that alerts the clone to stand up. The original man continues to see more clones with Apple Watches after he ventures outside, and they all run past him with far more energy than he has. The commercial culminates with a final clone sprinting past the original person and diving into the ocean for an intense swimming exercise.

The commercial highlights the fact that you *can* become a better version of yourself. While the commercial is meant to demonstrate how the Apple Watch can help you do that with respect to fitness, the principle of self-improvement applies to every conceivable facet of life. The fundamental premise of this book is that you can work toward becoming a better leader. The required changes do not have to be "revolutionary"—on the contrary, you can take incremental steps every day in order to improve yourself. For leaders in all school systems, every chapter in this book offers concrete steps that you can take to upgrade your abilities as an educational leader.

Becoming a better educational leader begins with the recognition that *the purpose of school is not just to teach students.* Rather, the purpose of school is to ensure that students *are learning.* That simple but, sadly, rare idea will already place you miles ahead of most leaders in this space. Instead of focusing on equipping and training teachers as the end goal, such efforts should instead be the *means* by which student learning is fostered. An effective leader will drive all organizational activity toward the singular goal of ensuring that students are learning.

An easy step that you can take in order to become a better leader is to increase your investment in the people around you. No man is an island, and your subordinates and colleagues will appreciate your acknowledgement of their role in the broader mission. When engaging with people, seek to *understand* rather than be *understood.* Your teachers especially will have important things to tell you, given that they are closest to the target of your entire enterprise—the students. Good leaders allow teachers to talk, but great leaders actually listen.

Once you recognize that school is about learning, and that you need to invest in your people, you need to ensure that your teachers are following through with the message. An effective leader will help his/her teachers in developing a learning environment for the students. Follow up with your teachers and emphasize their role in fostering a culture of fun, experiential learning. You'd be surprised by the number of leaders who remain "in the shadows," keeping their teachers at arm's length. Be available and be personable, and you'll be off to a great start.

You have the ability to transform yourself into a better leader by following the Leadership Cycle that I've detailed in these pages. Be the rare leader who respects the importance of details that many leaders would dismiss as "trivial." No matter what challenges your school faces, you have the tools, the knowledge, and the ability to tackle those challenges head on. You do not have to spend thousands of dollars on restructuring a program. You just need to tap into your most precious resource: time. Use that resource wisely, and go transform your school! Be the change, lead the change, and ensure the change! The future of student learning depends on it.

References

(1955). Statement: The Russell-Einstein Manifesto. *Pugwash Conferences on Science and World Affairs.* https://pugwash.org/1955/07/09/statement-manifesto/.

(2007). Robert Joss: "Leadership Is Not about You." *Stanford Graduate School of Business.* www.gsb.stanford.edu/insights/robert-joss-leadership-not-about-you.

Adams, Richard J. (1993). How Expert Pilots Think: Cognitive Processes in Expert Decision Making. *U.S. Department of Transportation Federal Aviation Administration.* http://www.tc.faa.gov/its/worldpac/techrpt/rd93-9.pdf.

Adams, R. J. & Ericsson, K. A.. (1992). Introduction to Cognitive Processes of Expert Pilots. *U.S. Department of Transportation Federal Aviation Administration.* http://www.tc.faa.gov/its/worldpac/techrpt/rd92-12.pdf.

America's Best Urban Schools Award Winners. (n.d.). *National Center for Urban School Transformation.* https://ncust.com/previous-americas-best-urban-schools-award-winners/.

Apple Watch commercial. (2018). Better You. *YouTube.* https://www.youtube.com/watch?v=0cBJBj_tbHM.

Ayivor, I. (2014). *Daily Drive 365: Daily Thoughts for Positive Living.* CreateSpace Independent Publishing Platform.

Blanchard, K. & Kearin, T. (2014). *Fit at Last: Look and Feel Better Once For All.* Berrett-Koehler Publishers.

Branch, G. F., Hanushek, E. A., & Rivkin, S. G. (2012). *Estimating the effect of leaders on public sector productivity: The case of school principals.* National Bureau of Economic Research.

Carlyle, T. (2015 reprint) *Goethe.* Palala Press.

Collins, J. (2001). *Good to Great: Why Some Companies Make the Leap and Others Don't.* Harper Business.

Coloroso, B. (2002). *Kids are worth it! Giving Your Child the Gift of Inner Discipline.* Harper Collins.

Consequence meaning. (n.d.) Your Dictionary. https://www.yourdictionary.com/consequence.

Consequence (n). (n.d.) Online Etymology Dictionary. https://www.etymonline.com/word/consequence.

Covey, S. (2004). *The 7 Habits of Highly Effective People: Powerful Lessons in Personal Change.* Free Press.

Dweck, C. (2007). *Mindset: The New Psychology of Success.* Ballantine Books.

Employee Job Satisfaction and Engagement Report. (2016). *Society for Human Resources Management* (SHRM). https://www.shrm.org/hr-today/trends-and-forecasting/research-and-surveys/pages/job-satisfaction-and-engagement-report-revitalizing-changing-workforce.aspx.

Fullan, M. (2008). *The Six Secrets of Change: What the Best Leaders Do To Help Their Organizations Survive and Thrive.* Jossey-Bass.

Ghanizadeh, A., & Moafian, F. (2010). The role of EFL teachers' emotional intelligence in their success. *ELT Journal: English Language Teaching Journal 64(4).* http://dx.doi.org/10.1093/elt/ccp084.

Ginsberg, S. (2012). *Consistency is Far Better than Rare Moments of Greatness*. HELLO! my name is Scott!

Goleman, D. (2011). *Leadership: The Power of Emotional Intelligence*. More Than Sound.

Goldsmith, M. (2007). *What Got You Here Won't Get You There: How Successful People Become Even More Successful*. Hachette.

Hattie, J. & Clarke, S. (2018). *Visible Learning: Feedback*. Routledge.

Heifez, R. & Laurie, D. L. (2001). The Work of Leadership. *Harvard Business Review*. https://hbr.org/2001/12/the-work-of-leadership.

Heifetz, R., Grashow, A. & Linsky, M. (2009). The Theory Behind the Practice: A Brief Introduction to the Adaptive Leadership Framework. *Harvard Business Press*. https://www.howardruff.com/ruff-quotes.

Holy Bible. (1978). New International Version (NIV).

Howard Ruff: Quotes to Live By.(n.d.)*Howard Ruff Legacy.*

Impelman, C. (2018). Never Mistake Activity for Achievement. *The Wooden Effect*. https://www.thewoodeneffect.com/activity-achievement/.

"I've Been to the Mountaintop" by Dr. Martin Luther King, Jr. (n. d.). *American Federation of State, County, and Municipal Employees* (AFSCME). https://www.afscme.org/about/history/mlk/mountaintop.

Johnson, Lady Bird. (2007 reprint). *A White House Diary.* University of Texas Press.

Kaplan, R.S. & Norton, D. P. (2005). The Office of Strategy Management. *Harvard Business Review*. https://hbr.org/2005/10/the-office-of-strategy-management.

Keague, S. (2012). *The Little Red Handbook of Public Speaking and Presenting*. CreateSpace Independent Publishing Platform.

King, M. L., Jr. (1960). "The Negro and the American Dream," Excerpt from Address at the Annual Freedom Mass Meeting of the North Carolina State Conference of Branches of the NAACP. *Stanford University.* https://kinginstitute.stanford.edu/king-papers/documents/negro-and-american-dream-excerpt-address-annual-freedom-mass-meeting-north.

Kiran, D. R. (2017). Seven Traditional Tools of TQM, in *Total Quality Management: Key Concepts and Case Studies.* https://doi.org/10.1016/B978-0-12-811035-5.00020-9.

Kotter, J. P. & Whitehead, L. A. (2010). *Buy-In: Saving Your Good Idea from Getting Shot Down.* Harvard Business Review Press.

Lynn, A. B. (2008). *The EQ interview: Finding employees with high emotional intelligence.* AMACOM/American Management Association.

Maurer, R. (2002). *Why Don't You Want What I Want? How to Win Support for Your Ideas without Hard Sell, Manipulation, or Power Plays.* Bard Press.

Maxwell, J. C. (2018). Tweet by @JohnCMaxwell. https://twitter.com/JohnCMaxwell/status/967069491686494209.

McDaniel, M. A., Hartman, N. S., Whetzel, D. L., & Grubb, W. L. (2007). Situational judgment tests, response instructions, and validity: A meta-analysis. *Personnel Psychology 60.* http://dx.doi.org/10.1111/j.1744-6570.2007.00065.x.

Millman, D. (2006). *Way of the Peaceful Warrior: A Book That Changes Lives.* H. J. Kramer.

Raymond, J. (2016). *Good Authority: How to Become the Leader Your Team is Waiting For.* IdeaPress.

Rosenthal, R. & Jacobson, L. (1968). Pygmalion in the Classroom. *The Urban Review 3.*

Reininger, M. (2012). Hometown disadvantage? It depends on where you're from: Teachers' location preferences and implications for staffing schools. *Educational Evaluation and Policy Analysis 34*. http://dx.doi.org/10.3102/0162373711420864.

Schwantes, M. (2021). Steve Jobs Once Gave Some Brilliant Management Advice on Hiring Top People. *Inc.* https://www.inc.com/marcel-schwantes/this-classic-quote-from-steve-jobs-about-hiring-employees-describes-what-great-leadership-looks-like.html.

Scott, S. (2004). *Fierce Conversations: Achieving Success at Work & in Life, One Conversation at a Time.* Berkley Books.

Seneca, L. A. (2018 reprint). *Moral Letters to Lucius: Epistulae Morales ad Lucilium.* Stadium Publishing.

Shinn, P. (2016). Superstars Bartoletta, Bowie, Gardner, Felix Sprint to Team USA's Second Straight 4X100-meter Gold. Team USA. https://www.teamusa.org/news/2016/august/19/superstars-bartoletta-bowie-gardner-felix-sprint-to-team-usas-second-straight-4x100meter-gold.

Summitt, P. (1999). Reach for the Summit: The Definite Dozen System for Succeeding at Everything You Do. *Currency.*

The 1963 March on Washington: A Quarter Million People and a Dream. (n.d.). *National Association for the Advancement of Colored People* (NAACP). https://naacp.org/find-resources/history-explained/1963-march-washington.

Whyte, William Hollingsworth. (1950). Is Anybody Listening? *Time.*